ART   IDEAS   HISTORY

FOUNDATIONS
OF
A NEW HUMANISM

1280-1440

GEORGES DUBY

SKIRA

TRANSLATED FROM THE FRENCH BY PETER PRICE

★

© 1966 by Editions d'Art Albert Skira, Geneva
Library of Congress Catalog Card Number: 66-15283

★

Distributed in the United States by
THE WORLD PUBLISHING COMPANY
2231 West 110th Street, Cleveland 2, Ohio

★

PRINTED IN SWITZERLAND

CONTENTS

I
VIA MODERNA

II
IMITATION OF CHRIST

III
POSSESSION OF THIS WORLD

I

VIA MODERNA

NEW MEN

During the fourteenth century the world of Latin Christianity showed a marked tendency to withdraw into its shell. It is true that the crusading fervor which had previously been the occasion for conquest had lost none of its compulsiveness and was still a guiding light both of ecclesiastical policy and of knightly conduct. But henceforward it was no more than a vision of what might have been. Between the years 1291, when Acre, the last Frankish possession in the Holy Land, was stormed, and 1396, when the Turkish army invading the Balkans routed the Crusaders at Nicopolis, there took place a gradual but unmistakable retreat from the eastern Mediterranean. After 1400 Byzantium was, in effect, a besieged and frightened outpost, doomed to succumb to the irresistible might of Asia and the Infidel.

This ebbing of the Western tide was due to the fact that the population of Europe, which for at least three hundred years had been steadily increasing, began to decline at the end of the thirteenth century. Before long the decline assumed disastrous proportions as a result of the Black Death in 1348-1350 and the numerous epidemics that followed it. By the beginning of the fifteenth century the population of many European countries was half what it had been a hundred years earlier. Countless fields lay fallow, thousands of villages were abandoned, and in most cities, as they shrank within their walls, whole districts fell into ruin. To this was added the tumult of war; for the aggressiveness which formerly had found vent in foreign conquest was now turned inwards. It led to constant clashes among States, great and small, by whose warring factions the unity of Christendom was shattered. Everywhere, in the open country and under the walls of besieged cities, the noise of battle could be heard. Armed bands of mercenaries and free companions looted and laid waste; brigands and freebooters made war their livelihood. The half-century on either side of the year 1300 witnessed one of the great reversals that have deflected, in physical terms, the course of

European civilization. The latter has followed two great rising curves, separated by a prolonged depression. The fourteenth century ushered in the era of stagnation and retreat that was to continue until about 1750.

This is no reason for echoing those historians who, unduly impressed by such evidence of recession, depopulation and strife, take an equally gloomy view of the history of thought, belief and artistic creativeness in the world of Latin Christianity. For there is no denying that cultural achievement in the fourteenth century, far from withering, was exceptionally prolific and progressive. The very decline and dislocation of physical amenities seem to have benefited cultural development in three ways.

In the first place, they altered the geographical distribution of wealth, thus creating new centers of intellectual and aesthetic activity. The effects of disease, battle and economic chaos were felt most severely in certain parts of Germany, in England and, doubtless more cruelly than anywhere else, in France, which had done especially well out of the earlier phase of expansion. Other regions, however, had emerged almost unscathed. In the Rhineland and Bohemia, in parts of the Iberian peninsula and above all in Lombardy, business was thriving, towns were expanding and a new spirit of curiosity and restlessness was abroad. As the seafarers from Genoa, Cadiz and Lisbon ventured further and further westwards, they began to shift the economic axis of Europe towards the Atlantic, thus making good all that had been lost in the Mediterranean.

Secondly, the misfortunes of the fourteenth century, especially the decline in population, were not invariably debilitating. They tended to concentrate wealth in fewer hands and to raise the general standard of living, thereby providing the means for more enterprising patronage of the arts and a wider diffusion of culture. At a time when successive disasters were scything away whole generations, men of substance seemed to be far thicker on the ground than they had been in the expansive calm of the thirteenth century, when the increase of wealth had not kept pace with that of the human race. As a result, more and more people began to indulge certain tastes and habits which formerly had pertained to the most select of the aristocracy. It became quite common for a man to drink wine or wear linen or read books; to decorate his house or his tomb, to appreciate a picture or a sermon, to commission an artist. Although production was stagnant and trade slumped, the love of luxury, far from weakening, was intensified.

Thirdly and above all, the collapse of the normal order of things eroded and undermined a number of values which had been the mainstay of Western civilization. Men's lives were in disarray, but they felt rejuvenated and, to some extent, emancipated. They were, indeed, exposed to greater suffering than their immediate forebears had known, but it was the stress and struggle of rejuvenation. The more percipient among them were struck, even dazzled by the feeling that they were living in a modern world and walking untrodden ways. They felt themselves to be new men.

Clear evidence of this sense of modernity may be seen in what happened to literary works composed around 1300, such as the second part of the *Roman de la Rose* or the incomparably more sublime *Divina Commedia*. Written in the vernacular for non-clerical readers, for whom they embodied all the learning and intellectual discoveries of the preceding age, these works helped to popularize culture, to broaden it down from schoolmen and clerics to intelligent laymen, especially those of the younger generation, who were eager to read and learn. They met with immense success. Expounded, discussed, read aloud in public, they became classics overnight. Their stock of knowledge and the way of life they portrayed became a yardstick for subsequent generations. They gave birth to literary criticism, which implied both aesthetic awareness and a feeling for the past, the sense of what had been and what was. At this time, in fact, every aspect of thought and sensibility underwent a process of renewal. It made itself felt in religion, for what came to be known, around 1380, as *devotio moderna* was the "modern" manner of approaching God. The constant, fundamental theme

of the new freedom consisted in opposition to the priestly hierarchy. In the fourteenth century European culture became popular and, *ipso facto*, secular. At this climacteric in the physical and spiritual history of Europe art kept up with the times by forsaking its emphasis on holy subjects. Henceforth its object was to provide men, in ever larger number, with the prospect or the recollection of pleasure.

*

Ars nova was the term used in the fourteenth century to designate certain types of music. Their main characteristics were profuse ornamentation, lack of didacticism, sheer aesthetic enjoyment and the attempt, accidental or contrived, to imbue sacred music with worldly delight. What happened was that instrumental flourishes were encroaching more and more on plainsong. Their burgeoning may be seen in the incidental music of Adam de la Halle or, much earlier, in the songs of the troubadours. Secular modes were invading the arcana of religious art, a process that was now being repeated in every realm of artistic creation.

No longer did architects, sculptors, goldsmiths, painters and those who employed them seek to swell the litany of the Incarnation which, during the thirteenth century, had gone forth from France throughout Europe, assigning to Man, Reason and Nature, those perfect expressions of God's presence, their true place in the harmony of creation. For these artists and their patrons, so determined to be modern, art was no longer, as it had been for the contemporaries of St Louis and as it would later become for the friends of Lorenzo the Magnificent, a means to lay bare the mysteries of the world and "our high-rais'd phantasie present." In their view art should merely depict, narrate, tell a tale. It should try to give a crystal-clear image of some story, or rather of a saga, not merely about God but also about the Knights of the Round Table or the Conquest of Jerusalem.

This was the essential change. The artist was no longer an acolyte, assisting the priest in his liturgical office. He had become the servant of ordinary men, men with eager eyes who wanted him to show them—not, indeed, everyday reality, for art became more than ever a means of escaping reality—but the world of their dreams. Hence the aim of fourteenth-century art was no longer to create a setting for prayer, ritual or Gregorian chant, but to capture dreams and make them visible. It was then that painting, since it could best give substance to a vision, won the primacy of the arts in Europe.

The motive power behind this profound transformation must be sought in the joint operation of three factors: social change, which affected the meaning and environment of artistry; change in beliefs and ideas, which affected the content and purpose of works of art; and change in the means of expression. Painters, like writers and philosophers, use a vocabulary inherited from the past and so deeply embedded in tradition that they can only break away from it slowly, painfully and with limited success. Something must be said, at the outset, about the nature of these three factors.

THE PATRONS

There is much to be said for beginning with the social aspects of art, for the new vitality and freedom of the fourteenth century were very largely the result of innovations in society. From the time when Europe became Christian down to the end of the thirteenth century, the major achievements in art, so vigorous that they endured and have left traces of themselves to the present day, were begotten of a single, very restricted class, whose members all shared the same outlook, education and aesthetic equipment. These men, who formed the exclusive coterie of the higher clergy, had been the true originators and unifiers of great liturgical art. After 1280, however, there was a considerable broadening of the social base of artistic achievement, which thus became more flexible, complex and heterogeneous. This process must be examined in some detail.

There was no marked change at this time in the artist's status. In the fourteenth century those who actually translated taste into works of art were all laymen; but so, for that matter, had been most of their predecessors in the twelfth and thirteenth centuries. They banded together in close-knit, highly specialized guilds, which became a sort of family, giving their members security, and helping them move from one town or place of employment to another, organizing meetings, training apprentices and propagating skills. They also, like all cliques, tended to become stereotyped and to be controlled by elderly men who looked askance at initiative. Such guilds already existed in the thirteenth century among goldsmiths and masons. After 1300 the system was simply extended to other crafts, such as painting. Sometimes it took the form of large, well-organized itinerant teams, artistic conquistadors, as it were, trained, led and inspired by a single chief in the person of a contractor who, like Giotto, sought commissions, made contracts and assigned jobs to his followers. Teams of this sort had, of course, worked long before on the building of cathedrals. It was only in the fourteenth century that the

leading works foremen, at the same time, indeed, as the *condottieri*, began to emerge from anonymity. They were asserting themselves and becoming known by name, which was the first step towards recognition of the creative personality. But even here the architects of the cathedrals had insisted on signing their work. Hence the only perceptible change consisted in extending a historical process which had also been shared by most types of craftsmanship. There was also the gradual rise in the status of painting, which was one of the major innovations in contemporary taste. The fact remains that until the end of the century, that is until the generation that reached creative maturity about 1420, the artist played second fiddle to his client. He was a manual worker of humble origin, generally one of the lesser townsfolk. His own skill was held in much lower esteem than the materials he worked in. Still, in the early years of the fourteenth century one begins to find artists of credit and renown who were eagerly courted and could sometimes pick and choose their clients. Such was Giotto, first of the great painters. Yet neither he nor even Ghiberti, a hundred years later, was wholly free. They were executants who could only deploy their skill in meticulous obedience.

One can, however, detect more definite changes in the relationship between the artist and those who paid him. At this time the art dealer made his first, hesitant appearance, in the sense that works were completed before being offered for sale. Shopkeepers would display them among their wares and leading Italian businessmen would make them known throughout Europe. This trade originated, no doubt, in articles like books, small ivory ornaments, devotional objects like traveling diptychs or gewgaws such as looking-glass covers or pouncet-boxes. There was even a trade in tombstones, for which Paris seems to have been the principal mart and place of manufacture. (But in Paris, too, in 1328 they were selling imported works of art, in the form of painted panels from Italy.) The steady boom in articles of virtu was stimulated by the fact that they were getting smaller and could more easily be transported. This in itself was only the corollary of a more fundamental stimulus: the fact that there was more money in private hands and that a growing number of citizens had the means and the inclination to buy things of beauty. No longer content with communal works of art, they wanted to have their own and to build up, for their enjoyment and credit, small-scale replicas of the treasures which formerly had been the prerogative of shrines and princes.

It was, in fact, this tendency to disseminate and secularize culture that made art a thriving business, and one can hardly exaggerate the part played by dealers in transforming the very conditions of artistic creation. Firstly, they brought a more rapid diffusion of methods and styles, with a resultant variety in contrast and cross-fertilization. But for the imported ivory figurines of Parisian workmanship, the sculptors, painters and goldsmiths of Central Italy would not have been so familiar with Gothic design. Secondly and above all, they set the artist free by transferring the initiative from client to creator. It must, however, be admitted that it was the lowest strata of creativeness that were thus emancipated. Only the seedier collectors went shopping, and what they found was the small change of art. There was little inventiveness in this reach-me-down stuff, where someone had dashed off a reproduction of a masterpiece, repeating it in a common accent. To reach the widest possible public, dealers sought primarily to lower the cost of production by speeding it up and using second-rate materials. When it came to turning out religious pictures, the fourteenth-century method was to strike them off by means of wood-engraving. Moreover, to attract and cater to these numerous purchasers, most of whom had little education, the retailers insisted on simpler, more obvious themes, with fewer demands on the intellect, greater appeal to the emotions and a larger element of story-telling. The part played by commerce in the art of this period was strictly that of making it popular. True creativeness found its stimulus elsewhere, in the activity of the patron.

Nowadays the really great artist, better off than any patron, has become his own patron. He composes and creates in total freedom, for his own enjoyment and as if for his own purposes. In these circumstances it is hard to realize how heavy was the yoke which, in the days of Cimabue, Master Theodoric or Sluter, the purchaser laid upon the artist. All major works were commissioned and every artist was rigidly subject to the will of his client, who might well be termed his master. This bond was of two kinds. Either there was a formal contract for a stipulated work, drawn up before a lawyer. This agreement specified, not merely the price and date of delivery, but the quality of the materials, the way in which the work was to be done and, last but not least, its general subject and layout, the colors to be used, the arrangement, gestures and appearances of the figures portrayed. Or else, in which case the loss of independence was more drastic and certainly more lasting, the artist spent some time as a member of his patron's domestic staff. Being part of his household and beholden to him for bed and board, or at best discharging the duties of a salaried employee, the artist was wholly at his patron's beck and call. This dependent status was, in fact, much sought after, for it freed a man from the restraints of belonging to a guild, a workshop or a team. Besides, it was the best way to make money. It put a man in touch with all that was most brilliant and up-to-date; it gave him access to the main centers of innovation, research and discovery; it set his feet on the ladder of social advancement. It is indeed in the aristocratic mansions of the early fifteenth century that one encounters a dawning respect for the artist's position and his freedom of action. Even so, the painter and sculptor, the carver of images and household goldsmith, even, in the grandest establishments, the overseer who directed the others and co-ordinated the work of embellishment, all bowed to the will of some lord. Can there conceivably have been any hint of give-and-take between him and the artist? Did Giotto argue with Enrico Scrovegni about any of the subjects for the Arena Chapel? Did the Limbourg brothers put before Jean de Berry their own designs for the calendar of the *Très Riches Heures*? The fact is that throughout the fourteenth century the meaning of an artist's work was wholly dictated, as a result either of his domestic status or of the terms of his contract, by the intention, taste or caprice of his patron.

The latter, of course, only imposed on the creative act its setting, theme and in a more limited sense, its mode of expression. The artist retained full control of his idiom, which had a life of its own, untrammeled by the dictates of patronage. This essential fact should be emphasized, for it emancipates the artist's work from its social context and explains why painters, sculptors and architects have always been discoverers and explorers of the universe. Like writers, scientists and philosophers, whom they sometimes anticipate, they have thus helped to give those who appreciate their work a new vision of the world. Needless to say there remained immense scope for individual inventiveness. Among all those captive artists there were many geniuses, and within the limits of their commission they gave free rein to their talents—more so, perhaps, than do modern artists who can choose their own subjects. The element of genius, of course, is impervious to analysis; but the aspects of a work of art that pertain to the history of taste and society were at that time controlled by its purchaser. He, therefore, is the proper object of this inquiry.

*

In the previous age art had flourished within a static, rigidly stratified society. The surplus wealth begotten of peasant labor flowed into the coffers of two restricted castes of nobility; one, warlike, and destructive, squandered its share in riotous living; that of the other, priestly and devout, was literally a sacrament to the greater glory of God. At the apex of these two élites stood the king, whose prowess in battle was combined, by virtue of holy unction, with the apostolic authority of a bishop. It was indeed the munificence of a king, St Louis, that brought the noblest art of the thirteenth century to its zenith. After 1280, however, the system began to break down. It is true that wealthy men were still addicted to habits of largesse and therefore to the patronage of artists, for oblations and rich gifts were doubly esteemed as symbolizing both power and humility. What changed was the character of patrons, and this was due in part to two influences.

The first of these trends consisted in a redistribution of wealth and a consequent dislocation and realignment of the ruling class which had the means to finance major artistic undertakings. There were two forces governing this trend. It resulted mainly from demographic change, especially the waves of high mortality that swept most of Europe in the second half of the century. In some areas epidemics,

beginning with the Black Death of 1348-1350, cut a swathe through the ranks of artists. In England the art of illumination, which up to then had been the country's outstanding and certainly most original achievement, suddenly deteriorated in the middle of the century and then went completely to seed. This was probably because the workshops were devastated by the plague and failed subsequently to repair their losses. Sometimes, therefore, high mortality may have had an immediate impact on the arts by annihilating the men who practised them. Yet it would seem that such a direct consequence was not usually widespread. No breach of continuity can be found in other sectors of English art, where the workers were doubtless more numerous and hardier. Thus the amazing originality of Gloucester Abbey flowered when the demographic disaster was at its worst. The death rate seems to have had a far deeper effect on the buyers of art and it was through them that it reacted on the themes and even the idioms of artists. For instance, there appears about 1350 an abrupt and striking change in the style of Central Italian painting. The stately elegance that lent such breadth and majesty to Giotto or Simone Martini suddenly vanishes and its place is taken by the comparatively vulgar mode of men like Andrea da Firenze or Taddeo Gaddi. There is no denying that work in the studios was disrupted by the sudden death of leading craftsmen and that it also suffered from the simultaneous upheaval in Florentine business, owing to the sensational bankruptcies that were the ruin of some and the making of others. The fact remains that the abrupt supersession of municipal authorities was unquestionably the decisive factor in the enervation of painting, its decline into prettiness, anecdote and gush. The plague of 1348, followed by recurrent epidemics, depleted the ranks of the upper class, who were already imbued with the humanist outlook. They were rapidly filled by jumped-up parvenus whose education was deficient, or at any rate markedly inferior, based as it was on the popular preaching of the Mendicant Orders. Art had to lower itself to their taste, with the result that, after 1350, the aesthetic standards of the Trecento in Tuscany, as indeed throughout Europe, declined in inverse ratio to the rate of social climbing.

Nor was plague the only cause of this scramble up the social ladder. It owed something to the fortunes of war, which at that time was endemic. It was not so much that the well-to-do suffered heavy casualties in battle, for they were adequately protected by the steady improvement in their armor. Besides, their opponents did not usually want to kill them but to take them alive. Fourteenth-century warfare was conducted with an eye to the main chance, in the form of ransom. Every knight who valued his fair name and put rank above the price of rubies secretly hoped, when he was taken prisoner, that his captor would set the ransom as high as possible. For such tangible proof of his consequence he would cheerfully undergo bankruptcy. Thus every battle and tournament involved large capital gains and losses. The victors, having done well out of their captures, often spent part of the windfall on artistic commissions. Lord Beaverly built his castle at Beverston with money wrung from French knights he had worsted in one of the big battles of the Hundred Years War. This particular English noble was already a wealthy man, and the fact that war, like the plague, opened the aristocracy to the low-born, sprung from a meaner, less cultivated class, was due to its becoming the business of professionals—captains, freebooters, *condottieri*, mercenary contractors of warfare. These people were quick to ape the manners and tastes of the nobility, but they made heavy weather of it in a plebeian, invariably ostentatious manner. Throughout the fourteenth century these two forces combined, by their exaltation of new men, to corrupt taste and lower aesthetic standards. Together they encouraged a general proneness to vulgarity.

The second major trend bore not on individuals but on society as a whole. Its effect was to change the circulation of property by upsetting the system of inheritance and causing the wealth necessary for patronage to flow into new channels. In the past all capital had consisted of land, in the shape of the rural manor yielding a fixed income. The most lucrative domains were, of course, those of the great religious houses, the monasteries, cathedral chapters and other ecclesiastical bodies who had promoted the highest achievements in art. After 1280 this scheme of things was disrupted by three factors. In the first place, the manorial system was affected by extensive changes in the farming economy which considerably impoverished the landowning aristocracy, and especially the old religious communities. Secondly, the royal States became much stronger and wealthier thanks to highly efficient fiscal innovations. About this time State taxation became the rule throughout Europe. By this means a large part of the currency in circulation was diverted to the royal coffers, where it provided the prince with luxuries, lined the pockets of his servants and financed the largesse to which he felt beholden not only by his own sense of dignity but also by the public image of Majesty which was now gaining ground. Thus while Christendom was contracting and growing weaker, the rare centers of great wealth constituted by royal courts could afford an increasingly brilliant display. This in itself favored yet a third tendency, whereby a number of big businessmen and financiers helped the sovereign with the levying of taxes and issue of currency. In this way they not only did well for themselves but contributed further to the glitter of the court. In most towns, which were losing their population, banking and commerce were on the wane; but they throve in the capitals and the principal marts where precious metals and luxuries were exchanged. Here the citizens of rank and fashion, enriched by services rendered at varying distance from the steps of the great thrones of Western Europe, acquired a taste for magnificence and largesse. At the same time they were becoming wealthy or cultivated enough to think of placing major commissions with artists.

These economic changes largely account for the fact that the Church's share in artistic activity steadily diminished during the fourteenth century. Ruined and exploited, crushed by royal and papal taxation, disorganized by changes in recruitment and the allocation of livings, nearly all the monastic and capitular communities ceased about this time to be major patrons of art. The only exceptions were a few churchmen and religious bodies, such as the Carthusians, the Celestines and the Mendicant Friars. Oddly enough, these were the most ascetic Orders, purporting to symbolize want and teach scorn for the flesh-pots. They ought seemingly to have condemned all forms of adornment and shown inveterate hostility to artistic creation. Some of them did. The Augustinian Eremitani who supervised Giotto's work on the Arena Chapel in Padua forced him to curtail his scheme of decoration and criticized him for doing many things "rather from pomp and self-seeking vainglory than for the glory and honor of God." Yet in the main the monasteries of the indigent Orders gave a great impetus to thirteenth-century art. There were two reasons for this. Being situated in or near large towns, they received lavish donations from nobles and citizens, for the abnegation and asceticism they exemplified won them the veneration of the inordinately rich, whose conscience was troubled by the life of ease and luxury they led. These communities, moreover, performed for society the important offices of preaching and burial, both of which called for a good deal of pomp and iconography. The fourteenth-century Church also produced individual patrons, such as abbots, canons, bishops, and, above all, cardinals and popes. In employing artists, however, these prelates did not act as ministers of religion or even as leaders of the community, but simply as men who wanted to cut a dash. In fact, they behaved exactly like princes. Apart from the indigent Orders, the Church's contribution to art was now in the hands of its most worldly, unspiritual members, those, in fact, who were already secularized. The bishops who beautified the cathedrals of England and France, though not princes themselves, were at any rate the servants of princes. They owed their wealth to the royal exchequer, just as the cardinals owed theirs to the papal treasury. They also inherited the tastes and ambitions of princes, especially the desire to exalt themselves by adding some signal and personal embellishment to their church. The lavish and fertile patronage of Boniface VIII at Rome or of Clement VI at Avignon, their encouragement of Giotto or Matteo da Viterbo were not intended so much to glorify God as to give spectacular and monumental evidence of their majesty in a State which was quite as much of this world as of the next.

Princes, in fact, took over from the Church the carrying out of major artistic projects, and their courts became the vanguard of creation and research. Of them all the most brilliant and powerful were those of the Pope, the King of France and the Emperor. They were, it is true, anointed rulers who since the dawn of Christian art had always been responsible for inspiring the finest artists. In the first place, however, it was during the fourteenth century that secular values began to prevail over religious in the interpretation of royal, papal and imperial authority, and that those who wielded it began to belittle their priestly function and to emphasize the *imperium*, that very concept of civil power which intellectuals were embracing as

they discovered the learning of ancient Rome. This was yet another facet of secularization. In the second place many of the wealthiest princes had never received holy unction and did not regard themselves in any way as priests. Such were the Duc d'Anjou, the Duc de Bourgogne, and the Duc de Berry who, as a result of the collapse of the French monarchy about 1400, had encouraged the revival of the Paris School; such too were the "tyrants" who had won control of the *signoria* in the great city-states of Northern Italy. In these courts, where men flocked and money flowed, with their travelers' tales and growing knowledge of the world, the social ladder could easily be climbed. They were the only place where the low-born could reach the highest rank, whether by military prowess, economic flair or clerical zeal. In these "households" and great families and courts, prayer was gradually giving way to policy, the spirit to the flesh. The new values were those of majesty and power, deriving in part from the Roman Law of jurists trained in the University law schools, partly from the Latin classics of scholars trained in the arts faculties. Even more conspicuous were the codes of chivalry and courtly behavior, products of the great development in social manners and observances which had begun with feudalism in the Middle Ages.

These scholarly and knightly values were adopted by the handful of prominent businessmen who in a number of towns, especially in Italy, were the only men outside the court and the cloister, capable of exercising a genuinely creative patronage. At that time the middle class in general did very little for the arts, and what it did was mainly on the lowest level of gimcrack production. Its patronage was organized communally through the innumerable brotherhoods to which the townsfolk belonged, their cultural activities being channeled into good works by the mendicant friars. It would be going too far, therefore, to claim that in the fourteenth century there was any middle-class art, or even middle-class taste. Only by rising above his class could the banker or merchant become a patron. This he did either by identifying himself with the court he served, or occasionally, in some of the great Italian cities, by helping to govern a municipal State and thus imparting to it not only the majesty and *imperium* of a prince but also the trappings of knightly decorum. All these men of substance, not to mention all sorts and conditions of townsfolk, were enthralled by what they glimpsed of courtly manners, with their combination of the ecclesiastical and aristocratic ideal. There was no "middle-class outlook," but rather a gradual permeation of a small group, sprung but emancipated from the middle class, by the courtliness of the knight combined with the humanism of the scholar. All this amounted as yet to a very slight broadening down but to a considerable degree of secularization.

One last consequence of social change must be stated. Wherever first-class art was appearing, whether in monastery, court or city-state, the new characteristics of fourteenth-century taste resulted in part from the greater initiative displayed by personal choice. This was true of objects bought in shops, ordered from a domestic artist or executed under contract. It was true even when the patron appeared to be a group, such as a civic guild, the chapter of York Minster, the Franciscans of Assisi or the Municipality of Florence. Always the decision turned on the purpose and taste of one man. When Giotto, in realizing the aesthetic ideals of the four-teenth-century Italian nobility, was at the height of his profession, he found himself confronted by a cardinal, Jacopo Gaetani dei Stefaneschi, and a pawnbroker's son, Enrico Scrovegni. He had to cope with them single-handed, and it seems unlikely, as we have pointed out, that he could bandy words. The artist nearly always had to serve one man, and a man with a far stronger personality than in the past and with far greater freedom to express it. This new-found freedom of self-expression, which pertained far more to the client than to the artist, is yet another facet of modernity.

The individual rather than collective origin of a work of art accounts for several characteristics that now began to emerge. In the first place, it showed much clearer evidence of personal affiliation. Even when it was public, in the sense of being offered to all and sundry, such as a stained-glass window or a statue over a church door, it always bore some outward stamp of having been made for this or that person. The ubiquity of heraldic symbols, the tendency of devotional paintings to include the figure of the donor, who presented them with a view to salvation for himself and his family, the attempt to make these figures true likenesses—all this is evidence of the patron's monopoly of the work he had initiated. The humbler his origins, moreover, the more jealous he was of his good name; and since the commission was a heaven-sent opportunity to show the world he had made good, he usually instructed the artist to be lavish in materials, layout and design. Fourteenth-century art, being dictated by private ambitions, tended to strain after effects and, in order to be more readily appropriated, to assume small proportions. Illuminated books, gold ornaments, jewels, valuable trinkets: such things could be handled, and by their costly materials they epitomized wealth and splendor. They appealed far more than a great statue or the vaulting of a nave to the taste of people who no longer wanted their aesthetic pleasures to be submerged in a community. Most of these objects now bore much more clearly the imprint of a personality. Usually it was that of the donor, who wanted to identify himself and to have certain details of his character brought out by the subject. Sometimes it was that of the artist, for the new patrons, who comprised fewer intellec-tuals than formerly, left greater initiative to the executant and allowed him more freedom of expression. Superficially, at any rate, the arts became more diversified, although at the bottom the artist's outlook, like that of his client, was still governed, throughout Europe and in every class, by certain cultural archetypes, common to them both.

In 1339 Jeanne d'Evreux, the widow of Charles IV of France, sought to acquire merit by making a benefaction to the royal abbey of Saint-Denis. She wanted her piety to take the form of a votive image of the Virgin Mother, standing in the traditional manner, with the Babe in her arms. The queen asked, however, that a more affectionate gesture by the infant Jesus should emphasize the Franciscan spirit of Love, and that her gift should be made of very costly material. The Parisian goldsmiths therefore made a small-scale model in silver-gilt, and they adorned the base, whose design gave a hint of church architecture, with a series of translucent, enameled scenes from the story of the Redemption. Personal ascription was modestly confined to a plain statement of the donor's name and rank, together with the exact date of her bequest.

About the same time Sir Geoffrey Luttrell of Inharm caused to be illuminated one of those psalters which corresponded in the devotions of the English aristocracy to the book of hours in France. On one page Luttrell appears himself in ceremonial guise. He has had himself portrayed in the rather crude trappings of knightly power, mounted for the tourney in a pose reminiscent of St George. He is attended by two fair ladies as evidence of his courtliness. The heraldic badge on his shield proclaims his prowess and that of his house.

In 1402 the humanist Pietro da Castelletto was commissioned by the heirs of that dashing prince, Gian Galeazzo Visconti, Duke of Milan, to write a funeral panegyric, which was illuminated by Michelino da Besozzo, pictor excellentissimus inter omnes pictores mundi. *The latter portrayed the dead man, surrounded by the abstract arabesques of courtly art, kneeling in his robes of State and bathed in the radiant presence of the Virgin and Child. Jesus himself is placing the diadem of the elect on his brow. The duchess, in a brocaded dress and holding a taper, stands in an attitude of mourning, while around her a group of fair maidens are in attendance upon Mary at the coronation. The gold background imbues the scene with the mystery of those dark, richly furnished closets where princes kept their treasure. Angels are holding aloft the various hatchments whose heraldic language proclaims the dead ruler's temporal power.*

By the end of the century donors were making their identity still more apparent by having effigies of themselves built into niches previously reserved for saints. They wanted to be recognized, for a good likeness immortalized their features and took the place of a mere symbol of ownership. About 1395 Count Pierre de Mortain gave a stained-glass window to the private chapel of the royal house of Navarre, in Evreux Cathedral. He is being presented to the Virgin by St Peter, his tutelary saint, and by St Denis, patron of the Kings of France, from whom he proudly claimed descent. He is fully armed, wearing his sword and the gilt spurs of knighthood. The surcoat of his cuirass is emblazoned with the insignia of his family. In order, however, that his features may be recognized, the artist has made them lifelike by transferring to glass the line drawing that would be used to illustrate a book.

Robert of Anjou made his oblation to the family saint, whose virtue had shed lustre on all the Angevin kings, and who afforded them from heaven his special protection. Here the living prince is glorifying his dead brother, who appears as a mightier prince than he. The bishop's throne has become a king's, and the penitential sackcloth worn by St Louis is almost hidden by a cloak as sumptuous as that of Robert himself. Angels are crowning the saint; the saint is crowning the donor. The path of intercession could not be more simply traced. The painting still displays the ancient hierarchy of worship. While it is true that Simone Martini has placed the two figures, one living and the other belonging to eternity, in the same majestic setting, it is evident that they come from different worlds. Later, however, when the Master of Flémalle was painting, realism had advanced so far that the picture had become a window, giving a glimpse of everyday life. One finds donors sharing the same surroundings and breathing the same atmosphere as figures from the other world. In the Annunciation *of the Mérode Altarpiece the donors are relegated to the courtyard, looking in upon the delightful abode of the Holy Family. For all their humility, there is something rather intrusive and tiresome about these bashful "extras." This, in fact, was the moment when the features of living men, which had entered into fourteenth-century religious art, began to withdraw from it and to emerge triumphant in the new-born art of portraiture.*

VIRGIN AND CHILD, 1339. SILVER-GILT STATUETTE GIVEN BY JEANNE D'EVREUX TO THE ABBEY OF SAINT-DENIS. LOUVRE, PARIS.

VIRGIN AND CHILD WITH BISHOP BERNARD D'ABBEVILLE, ABOUT 1268.
STAINED-GLASS WINDOW, AMIENS CATHEDRAL.

PIERRE DE NAVARRE, COMTE DE MORTAIN, KNEELING BEFORE THE VIRGIN, ABOUT 1395.
STAINED-GLASS WINDOW, EVREUX CATHEDRAL.

LUTTRELL PSALTER: SIR GEOFFREY LUTTRELL MOUNTED, ARMED, AND ATTENDED BY HIS WIFE AGNES AND HIS DAUGHTER-IN-LAW
BEATRICE. ABOUT 1335-1340. FOLIO 202 VERSO, ADD. MS 42130, BRITISH MUSEUM, LONDON.

MICHELINO DA BESOZZO. THE CROWNING OF GIAN GALEAZZO VISCONTI (DETAIL). MINIATURE FROM THE FUNERAL PANEGYRIC
OF GIAN GALEAZZO VISCONTI BY PIETRO DA CASTELLETTO, 1403. MS LAT. 5888, BIBLIOTHÈQUE NATIONALE, PARIS.

SIMONE MARTINI (ABOUT 1285-1344). ROBERT OF ANJOU, KING OF NAPLES, CROWNED BY HIS BROTHER ST LOUIS OF TOULOUSE, 1319-1320.
MUSEO DI CAPODIMONTE, NAPLES.

Duby III 8

MASTER OF FLÉMALLE (ACTIVE 1415-1430). THE MÉRODE ALTARPIECE, ABOUT 1420. THE ANNUNCIATION (CENTER) WITH DONORS (LEF

AND ST JOSEPH IN HIS WORKSHOP (RIGHT). THE METROPOLITAN MUSEUM OF ART, NEW YORK. THE CLOISTERS COLLECTION, PURCHASE.

THE WORLD OF THOUGHT

It is difficult and may well be impossible to determine precisely how changes in ideas, beliefs and social attitudes are related to new developments in art. In the case of the fourteenth century one is confronted by a mass of unknown quantities, for there was far less immediate connection between the two phenomena than there had been in the eleventh, twelfth or even thirteenth century, when the sole creators of great art had been learned men. It is evident that Saint-Denis faithfully reflects Suger's concept of the universe. The master-builders working on the abbey received explicit orders from him and it is fairly easy to see what he had in mind. In fact he expounded it himself, and there is no doubt that he planned and adorned the basilica just as he would have done a sermon and as, indeed, he planned and adorned his *Histoire de Louis VI le Gros*, using the same symbols, composing the same rhetorical and arithmetical harmonies, reasoning in a similar manner from analogy. On the other hand, while such pages from the *Très Riches Heures* as the *Garden of Paradise* undoubtedly reflect Jean de Berry's concept of the world, it is much harder to see how this happened. For one thing, the psychology of a French Prince of the Blood in 1400 is far more baffling than that of a twelfth-century Benedictine abbot. For another, his thought has undergone many subtle refinements.

It is true that much fourteenth-century art was intended to convey doctrine in a visual and intelligible form. This was true of all didactic pictures, especially the many paintings for which the Dominicans were responsible. The purpose of Andrea da Firenze's *Triumph of St Thomas Aquinas* in the Spanish Chapel at Santa Maria Novella in Florence, or Traini's painting of the same subject in Santa Caterina at Pisa, is not to depict Thomist philosophy and thereby restore it to public favor; it is rather to give people of average education a simplified version, all the more effective for being so easy to spell out, by reassuringly linking the philosophy, not only to divine wisdom, but also to such familiar "fathers" as Aristotle and Plato, St Augustine and Averroes. It was, however, exceptional for works to be so rigidly planned. The new forms of patronage were no longer so prone to doctrinaire influence. In most cases they reveal no more than a certain correspondence between the artist's product and a more or less sophisticated philosophy, according to the donor's rank. The subject, moreover, is less concerned with thought, belief or learning than with expressing some social custom, convention or taboo. As a result of its tendency to become popular and secular, fourteenth-century art no longer tried to "point a moral or adorn a tale." Instead it reflected cultural patterns that were supposed to display and vindicate the status of a much larger and more variegated public who, as self-appointed leaders of society, commissioned works from architects, sculptors and painters.

All, whether prince, prelate or banker, adopted the same cultural patterns, based on two contrasting ideals, two exemplars of wisdom and conduct: the knight and the priest. Since the dawn of chivalry at the end of the eleventh century these two figures had stood at the poles of human endeavor. Much fourteenth-century literature, such as the *Songe du Verger*, still took the form of a dialogue or disputation between the paladin of the Clergy and the paladin of Chivalry, upholding contradictory ideals and principles. One of the new features of this period was, however, the mingling of these two cultures. This resulted from various tendencies, beginning with social change. In the fourteenth century a growing number of men belonged to both worlds. The secular activities of priests led them to adopt worldly habits which formerly had been confined to warriors. Conversely, there arose a class of *milites literati* or "lettered" knights who could master book-learning and were avid of scholarship. This fusion was yet another product of the royal courts, where knights and clerics, being entrusted with the same missions, were expected to possess similar skills. The union of the two cultures found expression in a new, courtly literature, designed both to entertain the monarch and, in a wider and deeper sense, "to benefit his subjects," a form of publicity which was now becoming an important attribute of the royal prerogative. These books, being designed for a literate but not exclusively clerical readership, were no longer written in Latin. They combined scholastic learning with use of the vernacular.

The invasion of the Court by Scholasticism is most clearly evidenced by the profusion of translations. In Paris at the end of the thirteenth century one finds a first attempt being made, in the entourage of the King of France, to bring the Latin writings of the Schoolmen within reach of men who were knights by training and vocation. About this time Jean de Brienne adapted the military treatise by Vegetius and called it, significantly, *The Art of Chivalry.* Philippe le Bel had the *Consolation* of Boethius translated. His wife did the same for a discourse on love written two generations earlier, and so did his daughter-in-law for Ovid's *Metamorphoses.* Here one can detect a threefold tendency: in the case of the king, still conscious of his priestly role, a work on religious ethics; in that of the nobleman, "a verray parfit gentil knight," a technical treatise on the pursuit of arms; in that of the ladies, the rules of courtly love and their best classical authorities. After the middle of the fourteenth century the same movement developed still further under the aegis of Jean le Bon, of Charles V and his brothers. The cultural trappings of the knights and ladies at the French court were enriched by selections from such great scholars as Livy and Petrarch, St Augustine, Boccaccio and Aristotle, who had described the "properties of things" and disclosed the secrets of nature. All this may have been meagre, superficial and fragmentary, consisting of such snippets of elementary knowledge as best suited the minds and outlook of fashionable people. It was nonetheless a notable advance, and it was accompanied by another gradual ascent in the same direction.

At the end of the fourteenth century the Valois court and its attendant aristocracy began to be frequented by a group of humanists who were graduates of the universities and thereby connected with the Church. They gathered round a number of influential men who were employed by great nobles as amanuenses. This post, which had been created fifty years earlier in the papal court at Avignon, was something quite new in Paris. It spread throughout the capitals of Europe and the city republics of Italy. Since the secretary's main task was to draft his master's writings, he had to be an accomplished Latinist, well versed in the classics. The purely temporal character of his duties led him to examine secular Latin texts from a critical, aesthetic standpoint. To him they were no longer liturgical exercises or means of interpreting the Word of God; they had become political precepts, evidence of a past whose historical meaning was just beginning to be grasped and, above all, sources of earthly bliss and models of earthly virtue.

This change of outlook at so exalted a level, with all that it implied in terms of education and mental discipline, opened the way to a general deconsecration of ecclesiastical culture. This happened just at the time when a number of works, hitherto reserved for clerical instruction, were gaining currency in fashionable society. By adopting a popular and secular tone, the charmed circle of the court, which was both the apex of society and the cynosure of citizens and churchmen alike, helped to assimilate the knightly to the clerical outlook in everyday life. Meanwhile a similar coalescence was taking place at a deeper level, owing to structural changes in the two cultural patterns.

*

As regards knightly culture, it was a case of emphasis rather than change, for by becoming more coherent, more refined it gained in persuasiveness and influence, so that its essential creed of joy and optimism came to be widely adopted. The code of chivalry, with its ideal of the perfect knight as pictured in medieval poetry, reached its apogee in the fourteenth century, although its various tenets had long been in the making. The earliest of them, the most ingrained and tenacious, had already taken root among the French nobility when feudalism was emerging early in the eleventh century. This original foundation consisted of purely masculine and soldierly qualities: physical strength, valor, loyalty to one's chosen leader, together with derring-do, that hall-mark of courage and technical mastery which stamped the "parfit knight." In the fourteenth century the essence of chivalry was still delight in battle and conquest, in displaying ascendancy and riding one's high horse. A further set of values had been adopted, beginning among the French aristocracy, as a result of women's emergence from their lowly state. This occurred about 1100 in southwestern France. The warrior caste was obliged to give woman her due, especially the baron's wife and the Lady of the manor. This gave rise to a new set of conventions, rules of courtesy which every knight who valued his honor and good name was bound to observe. Relations between the sexes began to be governed by the European concept of Love. This code of love and war may well be summed up in the title of a book of madrigals by Monteverdi, *Canti guerrieri e amorosi*. They show, incidentally, that it was still flourishing in the age of Baroque. It found expression partly in poems extolling heroism and love; partly in the strategy whereby a man was expected not merely to vanquish his opponent but also to win and retain the love of his rival's Lady. In both cases this strategy originated and developed as a sport, albeit one which was directed by rigid respect for a code of honor.

By the end of the twelfth century the code had been perfected, and the literature of subsequent generations disseminated its precepts throughout Europe, among men who wished to achieve distinction. Even before 1200 a number of major works had appeared, embodying such paladins of knightly legend as Perceval and King Arthur; but the height of their success and influence on society dates from the fourteenth century. It was at this stage in European civilization that the ruling class became intoxicated by knightly epics, which portray it at its most flamboyant by means of an increasingly stylized ritual, totally divorced from normal behavior. The fourteenth century was really an age of bloody warfare, arson, butchery and rape, when battlements bristled with spears amid a desolate, ravaged landscape, so brilliantly depicted by Simone Martini in the background to his equestrian portrait of a *condottiere*. The latter, however, fancied himself as a knight and pranced on the battlefield in all his finery. Yet at Crécy, Poitiers and Agincourt the nobles most wedded to chivalry made it a point of honor to fight in a courtly manner. Blind princes had themselves tied to the saddle and guided to the thickest of the fray, there to die gloriously like the heroes of Lancelot. At court even the most bloodstained mercenaries paid their suit to fair princesses. Just as

the old nobility were being ruined by economic change and their place usurped by self-made men who had done well out of war, business or service in some royal household, so the old prerogatives were being replaced by hollow, artificial replicas, which nonetheless kept the system in being. Such were the orders of chivalry founded in the fourteenth century by the kings of Castile, France and England, by the Emperor and the Dauphin of Vienne, as well as by many lesser princes, with a view to recreating King Arthur's Round Table. The new men could only become socially acceptable by showing how good they were at making love and war and how meticulously they observed the rules of the game. The real liturgy of the age, and the only one that still commanded respect, consisted in Courtesy and Prowess. They were displayed at galas and festivities, of which warfare was as much a part as any ball or tourney. That is why fourteenth-century art was no longer inspired by holy rubric but began to reflect these secular rites, giving them greater reality and enhancing their success. The sumptuous portrayal of knightly culture is, perhaps, the most striking innovation in art at this time.

From the outset chivalry had implied certain values that linked it to priestly culture. It had also, like all other social relationships, been subject in feudal times to evangelical pressure by the Church. A number of soldierly qualities, such as energy and prudence, had much in common with theological virtues. But churchmen went a good deal farther than this. Eleventh-century Christianity was so eager to trim its sails to the prevailing winds of society that it sanctified aggression. The Crusade was the Christian apologia for military prowess. Nonetheless, while the Church countenanced warfare, feats of arms and massacres, it continued to frown upon the pursuit of earthly joy, for which chivalry and courtliness were so largely responsible. The knight despised gold and commercial utility as heartily as any monk; but he did so in order to revel in waste, luxury and riotous living. Courtly love, of course, being rooted in adultery and lust, seemed no more compatible than military aggressiveness with Holy Writ. In this case, after some attempts to channel it in the direction of mariolatry, the Church refused its benediction. The literature of chivalry in the thirteenth century proclaimed the conflict between the exponents of ascetic and penitential Christianity, whom it denounced as canting sabbatarians, and the true knights, who sought to reconcile an easy-going belief in redemption with their love of life in this world. This contrast is made ironically in *Aucassin and Nicolette*, brutally in the songs of Rutebeuf, and with guileless freedom by Joinville.

At the same time, however, the knightly spirit of cheerfulness had worked its way into priestly culture. In one sector of Christianity it had sown the seed of revolutionary change. Before his conversion Francis of Assisi, the son of a prosperous citizen, had been steeped in the courtly ideal. Like other young men of his class, he had dreamed of knightly adventures and had written gay ditties. At the beginning of the thirteenth century, when, like a lovesick swain, he chose poverty for his Lady, he did so in the hope of attaining perfect bliss in accordance with the courtly code. Franciscan Christianity, more in keeping with the Gospel than any other, is fundamentally and deliberately optimistic. Triumphant and lyrical, it seeks the harmony of creation and proclaims the goodness and beauty of God in the love of all living things. The Franciscans accept all the most exacting demands of Christianity; yet they do not reject the world but go out to meet and conquer it. In this way they have adopted all that is most buoyant in the code of chivalry. The message of St Francis was too novel, too revolutionary to win complete acceptance from the Catholic authorities, and much of it was frittered away in the course of the thirteenth century. What remained, however, pervaded the world of religion, influencing the Church far beyond the Mendicant Orders and even winning over the rival host of Preaching Friars. In the fourteenth century, when theologians came to believe that every creature contained a spark of divinity and was worthy of love and consideration, they were following where the Poverello had led. So, too, was the Dominican, Heinrich Suso, when he extolled God in a paean of thanksgiving reminiscent of the *Laudes creaturarum*: "Most worshipful Lord, I am not worthy to adore Thee, yet my soul yearns for the heavens to sing Thy praises when they are lit in all their enchanting loveliness by the lamp of the sun and by the shining multitude of stars. Let the meadows extol Thee when high summer burnishes them in natural splendor, when they are enameled with bright flowers and attired in their own exquisite grace." Thanks to the teaching of St Francis, such feelings were brought into harmony with the code of chivalry and courtliness, which ceased to be merely the criterion of civilized behavior in Europe and set its seal on the new outlook of the Church.

*

The secular spirit entered the academic world of professional theology by a different channel. In the principal towns of Europe merchants had founded small grammar schools where their sons could be taught enough of the three R's to carry on the family business. Apart from these, teaching and learning were still clerical functions and the universities were in the hands of the Church, who claimed both students and masters for her own. Not all of them, however, intended to become priests, and some faculties, constituting the least clerical part of the university, trained men for lay professions. For at least two hundred years some of them—it was a speciality of the Bologna Law School—had offered facilities for reading and expounding Roman law. Here Scholastic logic could be applied to strictly temporal problems, those of government especially. These faculties forged the weapons of a political science unencumbered by theocracy, which asserted the secular supremacy of the Emperor and was inclined to contest the Church's claim to temporal sovereignty over the world. Since 1200 they had gradually been discovering ancient Rome, its laws, its symbols and some of its virtues. Owing to the increasing power of the state and its need for a larger and better trained staff of servants, the study of law became steadily more important, and with it that part of university life which was most attracted by secular modes of thought.

The biggest changes, however, occurred in those seats of Christian learning and nurseries of preachers and prelates, the Divinity Schools of Paris and Oxford. The vital stroke that was to free learning from its bonds was delivered in 1277, when an ecclesiastical ukase, first in Paris and then at Oxford, forbade the teaching of Averroes, the expositor of Aristotle, thereby condemning certain postulates of St Thomas Aquinas. This cast a slur on the efforts made during the past fifty years by the Dominicans of Paris to bring Aristotelian philosophy into line with Christianity, thus achieving the concordance of faith and reason which had been the goal of Latin Christianity since the end of the eleventh century. The Dominicans retorted at the General Chapters of 1309 and 1313, forbidding any departure by their members from Thomist doctrine. In 1323 they secured the canonization of St Thomas, and they sought by every means, especially painting, to vindicate him in the eyes of all men. They were successful in Italy, where throughout the fourteenth century the universities remained faithful to the teaching of Aristotle and the traditional methods of Scholasticism. In Paris and Oxford, however, their position was sufficiently undermined for the initiative in theological inquiry to pass, about 1300, to their rivals, the Franciscans. A revolution in Christian thought was accomplished by two Friars Minor, English scholars trained at Oxford, where for some time the emphasis in teaching had lain on mathematics and the observation of phenomena. Hitherto the aim had been to elucidate revealed truths by the rational methods of Aristotelian logic. Duns Scotus pointed out that only a very small part of dogma could be established by reason; the remainder must be taken on trust and no attempt should be made to prove it. After him, William of Occam really initiated the "modern approach." He stood in direct opposition to Aristotle, for he held that concepts were symbols and had no intrinsic reality, that cognition could only be personal and intuitive, and that the attempt to reach God or understand the world by means of abstract reasoning was futile. Man could only do so by two distinct paths: either by an act of faith, entailing acceptance of such undemonstrable truths as the existence of God or the immortality of the soul; or by logical deduction applied solely to what could be directly observed in the physical world.

Occamist doctrine went hand in hand with the tendency of civilization to become secular and thus inspired the whole of western thought in the latter part of the fourteenth century. It indicates two ways of evading the restraints of the Church. In the first place, by insisting on the non-rational character of dogma, it made possible an approach to God through love instead of reason. This released the powerful spring of mysticism which had welled up in Latin Christianity since the days of St Augustine, but which the triumph of Scholasticism had checked, forcing it back into the cloisters of Franciscan monasteries and small communities of ascetic penitents. It was thanks to this strain of mysticism that fourteenth-century Christianity made such a

wide and powerful appeal to the weak and ignorant, to humble folk and women. By substituting the individual for the community religion emancipated itself from the clergy. The supreme act of devotion now consisted in a loving quest for God, in the hope of union and fusion, of "marriage" between the quintessence of the human soul, the "ground" of Meister Eckhart, and the divine substance. In this private dialogue the priest had lost something of his liturgical function, for the believer could not authorize others to pray for him. He must himself attain gradually to the state of inward enlightenment, by means of spiritual exercises, immediate contact with Holy Writ and the daily imitation of Christ. It no longer behoved the priest to teach or expound; he was no more than a mediator, who should bestow sacramental grace and bear witness to Christ. On the other hand, more was expected of him and there was more awareness of anything in his attitude to "the pomp and vanity of this wicked world" that might seem inconsonant with his office. Occamism gave a foothold to those who attacked the Church for daring to poach on secular preserves; to those who sought to bridle its ambition and denounce clerics who were profligate or unchaste; and also to those who wanted the hierarchy to be amenable in disciplinary matters to the civil power and restricted by it to a purely spiritual role.

In the second place, when William of Occam encouraged men to unveil the mysteries of the physical world by reasoning from their experience, he was proclaiming the total freedom of scientific inquiry. Occamism consists above all in the rigid segregation of sacred and profane. The former is the province of the heart and should be under the spiritual direction of a purified Church. The latter belongs to the intellect and must be exempt from priestly interference. This doctrine not only secularizes knowledge but frees it from all metaphysics, especially from "Aristotle and his philosophye." It was not long before a Parisian scholar, Nicolas d'Autrecourt, could assert: "There is a degree of certainty that men can attain if they apply their minds, not to the Philosopher or the Commentator, but to the study of things." The new approach was immensely stimulating when it led to all strange phenomena being observed directly, critically and without reference to any preconceived system. It resulted in their being portrayed as they really were, in all their diversity, and in the replacement of the abstract, conceptual symbol by the true image of this or that creature. In this way Occamism gave an impetus towards realistic art. The growing realism of painting and sculpture in the fourteenth century should not be ascribed to the development of a mythical "bourgeois spirit." We have seen that the art of that time did not originate with the bourgeoisie. Realism in fact had its vanguard in the great aristocratic households, where the leading artists and scholars lived on intimate terms; and it kept pace with the most enlightened aspects of academic thought.

The development of philosophy had much in common with the propensity of chivalry no longer to belittle the tangible world and its phenomena, but to consider them excellent and worthy of notice. This characteristic shared by the two cultures required a more optimistic appraisal of creation, of a civilization which in the eyes of some was collapsing into ruin, and of a more variegated, fluctuating society where education and personal religious experience were rapidly gaining ground. The fourteenth century owes much of its modernity to this optimism and heightened awareness of things. It remained to find an idiom capable of expressing them.

1

THE SPIRIT OF CHIVALRY
AND THE CONCEPT OF SPACE

Like the liturgical world of the cathedrals, the world of chivalry was governed by myth and ritual. Prowess, largesse and courtesy were the values it set store by—values exemplified by King Arthur, Charlemagne and Godefroi de Bouillon. These paragons of the knightly virtues were not dream figures; they had once lived among men. Now, however, they no longer belonged to history but rather to legend, and the memory of their deeds set chronology at naught. They stood outside the pale of time. They figured regularly in the symbolic representations which accompanied the ordered rites of court ceremonial, coronation festivities, jousting and courtly love. In these plays they stood not only outside time but moved in an imaginary space, a fictive world without any limits or fixed dimensions. The central theme of the myth was the perilous adventure, the wandering quest, which led the heroes of chivalry—and the living actors who momentarily mimed their actions—into the indeterminate depths of the forest.

Of all the forms of nature, the forest offered the most favorable setting for the incidents of romantic fiction and the vicissitudes of clandestine lovers. Its shadowy glades and pathless depths conjured up an atmosphere of mystery and suspense which effectively blurred the dividing line between reality and fantasy.

The tapestries known in France as *verdures*, patterned with flowers and foliage, brought forest scenery into the halls of fourteenth-century castles and manor-houses. Similar designs, suggestive of the shifting, amorphous space of myth and romance, appeared in the ribs of Gothic vaulting and in the margins of illuminated manuscripts.

By about 1300 the ornamentation of the great cathedrals had been completed. Here the spirit of chivalry prevailed over the logic of the builders. Logic was lost to sight beneath an overlay of ornaments in which the fanciful and irrational were given free play. Thus in the central doorway of Rheims Cathedral the traditional scene of the Coronation of the Virgin stands detached from the façade; drifting away from the stability of the main fabric, it floats up into a dream-space. The natural upward thrust of Gothic churches is here released from measurable dimensions, soaring up in a profusion of flower and foliage ornament clinging to the edge of the gable. At the apex, borne on the wings of angels, the sun itself turns into a flower. These forms shoot up like the tree of the forest, like the flashing of light as it was conceived in the Franciscan cosmology of the Oxford schools. It was this vigorous burgeoning which, in the vaulting of Tewkesbury Abbey, in the octagonal crossing of Ely Cathedral and in the chapter house of Wells Cathedral, disrupted that ordered plenitude of space of which the master-builders of the thirteenth-century had found the principles in Aristotelian physics.

The illogical space of the forest, that ideal setting for knightly adventure and romance, also invaded the pages of English illuminated manuscripts, where it brought about a return to the fantasy of Celtic and Anglo-Saxon miniatures. Take, for example, the illustration to Psalm 109 in the psalter of Robert of Ormesby, a monk of Norwich. The large initial D encloses the symmetrical figures of God the Father and Christ the Son in a space which is still as rigorously ordered as that of a stained-glass window. But already in the foliage border surrounding the text the artist has given free rein to his fancy. The plant motifs, sprouting in all directions, teem with exquisitely rendered specimens of animal life, including the dragons which knights were always slaying in the recesses of the forest, though the stag was their usual game.

In Paris, however, the logic of the preaching friars of the University was still too strong for book illuminators to go as far as this. Produced about 1325 under Dominican influence, the Belleville Breviary illuminated in the workshop of Jean Pucelle has its margins sparingly decorated with leafy stems kept well under control, their pure arabesques standing out against the blank space around them. As for the decoration of initial letters, no great play is made with the abstract form of the letter. The essential thing is the scene it encloses within a pattern of sober lines where air circulates freely; this space is that of Giotto's pictorial staging. The painter who, half a century later, illuminated the *Grandes Chroniques de France* also placed the actors in the coronation ceremony on a kind of stage. But here it is the sinuous grace of the figures themselves that brings to mind forest trees and climbing plants.

Lorenzo Monaco, a Camaldulese monk, was at work in Florence at the very time, in the early fifteenth century, when Masaccio was painting his great frescoes in the Brancacci Chapel with their austere and stoic figures. Masaccio created a new language of art which few of his contemporaries could understand; whereas most of the Florentine patricians responded at once to Lorenzo's Gothic charm and courtly refinements. To the dramatic pathos of the Gospel story he gave an exotic appeal wholly in the spirit of the age of chivalry; his hallucinated Magi go riding through a rocky wilderness towards a land of dreams.

THE TREATMENT OF SPACE IN ITALIAN PAINTING

Having emerged triumphant at the end of the thirteenth century, the Popes were determined to lay their yoke on the Franciscans and bring them within the normal hierarchy. They therefore summoned the best artists in Italy to Assisi, so that the new message of the Friars Minor might be painted under the supervision of the Cardinals who were patrons of the Order. It was hoped that, if the main events of the Gospel story were thus brought to life, ordinary men and women would be stirred to the depths of their being. Cimabue, therefore, took the stiff, conventional figures of the Passion and filled them with a dramatic frenzy, whose daemonic power and anguish have only been enhanced for us by the ravages of time.

Then Boniface VIII wanted St Francis to be depicted in the Upper Basilica as the protector of the Roman Church. He summoned Giotto and told him to illustrate a number of passages from the Poverello's official biography. This the painter did by means of a frieze of separate but related scenes, cut off by a frame from their architectural surroundings. Later, in the Arena (or Scrovegni) Chapel at Padua, he used the same method to tell the life-story of Christ, the Virgin and Joachim.

In Giotto one finds none of the boundless horizons beloved of knightly romance. He divided space and time into strict compartments which, though also unreal, had the unreality of the theater. His settings were so designed as to leave room for actors to move freely, group themselves or give full rein to gesture and mime. In this way he created a space between the spectator and the backdrop of a classical proscenium, deep enough for the episode to be fully enacted. A little symbolic scenery provided a muted accompaniment, but what mattered was the action. The artificial setting removed the characters from their ordinary world to the empyrean of sacred drama. There they stood forth, St Francis and his friends, Joachim and the shepherds—and so did Mary and Jesus—depicted in the full reality of flesh and blood.

A hundred years later, a number of leading Florentine citizens came under the influence of humanists like Coluccio Salutati and Niccolò de' Niccoli. They spurned both the fevered effusions of mysticism and the dreamy make-believe of chivalry. With a Roman emphasis on the dignity of man, they aspired after a Christian faith no less deep and ardent, but sterner, untroubled by emotion and imbued with the sedate austerity of the Stoics.

Thus when Masaccio painted the Florentine chapel for whose decoration the silk-merchant, Felix Brancacci, had provided in his will, in 1422, he took his inspiration from Giotto. He created a space uncluttered by superfluous ornament and gave it depth by means of an architectural setting. There he placed the marmoreal figures of the apostles Peter and John, giving alms to the poor with the aloof deliberateness of human benevolence.

Between 1337 and 1339 Ambrogio Lorenzetti had the task of depicting, in the Council Chamber at Siena, the allegory of Good Government with its attendant Virtues, and of portraying the twenty-four City Fathers. He placed his figures, as it were, on the two tiers of a stage, and a very narrow one at that. Since he had a message to impart, he employed symbols and explanatory texts. The clearly demarcated space was itself symbolic of the new proselytizing zeal of the Preaching Friars. Beneath this imaginary scene, however, Ambrogio painted the vast expanse of Sienese contado, *without any artificial boundary—neither the architectural trimmings usually placed round Gothic pictures nor the little* trompe-l'œil *columns of Assisi. Ambrogio's space is as crowded as Aristotle's, for the landscape runs up to an excessively lofty horizon, practically shutting out the sky; yet it is a real landscape, for it was painted for a community of merchants and vine-growers, men who knew the price of a sack of corn or a bale of wool.*

There is no fear of those falconers getting lost in the greenwood. Every tree stands out by itself, as if it were the Idea of a tree. This is not the space of dreams or rites or the theater, or even that of idealized Virtues; it is the space of common sense, public policy and hard work. It was intended for men who built town clocks to divide up the day into hours, men who wanted to see where they were going and how much they were making.

CIMABUE (ACTIVE 1272-1302). THE CRUCIFIXION, ABOUT 1277. FRESCO, UPPER CHURCH OF SAN FRANCESCO, ASSISI.

AMBROGIO LORENZETTI (ACTIVE 1324-1348). THE EFFECTS O

GHERARDO STARNINA (ABOUT 1354-1413). ANCHORITES IN THE THEBAID (DETAIL).
UFFIZI, FLORENCE.

...OOD GOVERNMENT, 1337-1339. FRESCO, PALAZZO PUBBLICO, SIENA.

GIOTTO (ABOUT 1266-1337). ST FRANCIS RENOUNCING THE WORLD AND THE DREAM OF POPE INNOCENT III, 1296-1297. FRESCO, UPPER CHURCH OF SAN FRANCESCO, ASSISI.

GIOTTO (ABOUT 1266-1337). JOACHIM WITH THE SHEPHERDS, 1305-1306.
FRESCO, ARENA CHAPEL, PADUA.

MASACCIO (1401-1429). ST PETER AND ST JOHN DISTRIBUTING ALMS, 1426-1427.
FRESCO IN THE BRANCACCI CHAPEL, SANTA MARIA DEL CARMINE, FLORENCE.

NEW MODES OF EXPRESSION

In order to symbolize what was invisible, divine reason and the conceptual order of the universe, Latin Christianity had recently devised a language so splendid that it constituted a formidable obstacle to change. The works executed in thirteenth-century Paris by St Louis had perfected the art of translating the mystery of the Incarnation into stained glass and stone. Having reached its apogee, Parisian Gothic became crystallized in simple formulae, so satisfying that they discouraged all attempts at innovation and resulted in inertia. During the fifty years after the Sainte-Chapelle was completed, Parisian artists seemed to be imprisoned in a style which they were incapable of adapting to changes in thought and the outlook of civilized society. At a time when Boethius was being translated for Philippe le Bel, when Duns Scotus was teaching at Paris, when William of Occam was working out his system, the master-craftsmen, stone-cutters, glassmakers and illuminators continued to depict the messianic universe of Albertus Magnus, Perrotin, and Robert de Sorbon. Thanks to the influence of the University of Paris, where all professional thinkers were trained, the thriving trade in illuminated books and ivory statuettes carried these designs all over Europe. Yet the idea they gave of the world was already out of date.

At the beginning of the fourteenth century a modernizing current began to flow from two directions. French Gothic itself began to show a gradual but marked proclivity to mannerism. Patrons, becoming more susceptible to luxury and worldliness, began to insist on elegance. Artists tried to meet their wishes by diluting the pure Gothic style with a degree of concettism. They used costlier, more gratifying materials; they added frills to the sober masses of rational architecture; above all, they played tricks with design. By elaborating the arabesques that came from the partitioning of stained glass and from the clean lines of monumental statues, the blithe spirit of courtliness invaded and soon burst asunder the symmetry of liturgical art. Graceful and fine-spun, the arabesque used the swelling curves of statues or, still more freely, the lush foliation in the margin of illuminated books to interpret the rites of fashion which were gradually superseding those of divine worship. As a counterpart to the rhythm of rounds and virelays, to the preening of courtship, to the vicissitudes of the knight-errant's quest, these modulations reflected the dreams and various moods of courtly society, its desire for elegance, its gay pursuit of pleasure and adventure, its incipient frowardness in love. At the same time, to link this poetic fiction with reality, the breaks and flourishes of its design, like the harmonic breaks and intervals of the *ars nova*, must contain some identifiable and meticulously observed elements of reality. French artists, therefore, took example from sculptors who, on the capitals of cathedrals, had faithfully reproduced the foliage of gardens and coppices in the Ile-de-France. They also adapted the more recent experience of monumental masons whose clients asked that sepulchral effigies should be true portraits of the dead. Fully to express courtly fantasy, they had to combine symbol, allegory and an illusion of realism. By about 1320 they succeeded in eliciting from classical Gothic a lively, mannered style which by unexpected twists, like the discourse of a dream, wove fragments of plain truth against a background of myth and outlandishness.

At the same time, echoes of even more revolutionary changes were coming from Central Italy, whose merchants and bankers had got control of all the most lucrative business in Europe. Changes in Western economy had combined with the new system of papal taxation to make this region the financial power-house of the continent. Thanks to this accumulated wealth Paris was confronted by a rival in artistic creativeness and originality of expression. Although Italy had felt the preponderance of Parisian design, backed up by the expanding importation of French products, this subjection was more apparent than real. Her aesthetic tradition rested on two massive foundations. One was the bounty of the East, that glorious mantle of mosaics and icons which Byzantium had bestowed on Italy, layer upon layer, throughout the high noon of the Middle Ages and down to the twelfth century. It was still a living tradition, linked to its source by the trade-routes that ran between this part of Europe and Constantinople, the Black Sea, Cyprus and the Morea. The other foundation, deeper still, was indeed the bedrock of the Italian people: ancient Rome, whose ruins lay all around and many of whose buildings had survived. It might even be traced back to the remote Etruscans. Backed by the wealth of the Holy See and of the cardinals who patronized the order of St Francis and were themselves subsidized by the businessmen of Siena and Florence, the new artistic movement broke away from Paris. It rejected the alien and supposedly colonial influence of Byzantium and, striking down to the tap-roots of the Roman world, it proclaimed allegiance to the Italian motherland by reviving the forms of antiquity. It was indeed a Risorgimento, whose hero was Giotto. At the time when Dante was electing to write the *Divine Comedy* in Tuscan, it was Giotto who, according to the earliest critic of his art, the fourteenth-century Florentine painter, Cennino Cennini, changed "the art of painting from Greek to Latin." He changed it, that is, from a foreign tongue to an indigenous vernacular. Giotto had, in fact, been anticipated by sculptors who, working for Frederick II about the middle of the thirteenth century, had resurrected in Campania the style of imperial Rome. They were followed by the sculptors of Pisa, still rich from "holding the gorgeous East in fee," a city more imperial than Rome itself, where the German kings passed on their way to receive the imperial diadem in Rome. It was here that the Emperors fell foul of the Popes. Nicola Pisano, when decorating the pulpit of the Baptistery in 1260, designed a replica of an ancient sarcophagus. In the apse of the Cathedral, Pisa was placed in effigy as Queen Mother beside the Emperor, kneeling before the Virgin. Later, as the base of the pulpit he carved about 1310, Giovanni Pisano used a statue of the city, supported by four Virtues, facing one of the Emperor supported by the Evangelists. Civic pride united with devotion to the Empire to bring about a revival of Roman statuary.

Thus, early fourteenth-century art adopted two new modes of expression. In France it was all sunny charm, willowy grace and unconstraint, such as one sees in the *Eros* at Auxerre or the *Tempter* at Strasbourg. In Tuscany, Umbria and Rome itself, there was a sterner note of stateliness and secular power. Both made their first appearance in stone-carving; but since art was tending more and more towards narrative and description, they soon found their fullest expression in painting. Both reflected the intrusion of secular values. But the new Gothic style implied no more than a gradual change in conventions: the infiltration of knightly and courtly manners into regal and ecclesiastical ceremony; the permeation of worship by Franciscan gaiety and the steady renewal of respect for God's creatures. The Roman manner, on the other hand, represented a far more drastic departure. There was no gradual change in the triumphant Italy of Imperial Vicars and Princes of the Church; in the Italy of the *podestà* and the *condottiere*, of usurers and guilds and cities "branchy between towers" and hills that were becoming a vast amphitheatre of terraced fields, olive-groves and vineyards. Here the language of art underwent a seismic upheaval. The kings of Europe whose finery was supplied by Italian merchants; the pilgrims who flocked to Rome; the princes of France or Germany who went to Italy in search of fame and fortune: all experienced a far more blatant worldliness. In classical models Italian painters found the formula of a *trompe-l'œil* realism that accentuated the futility of symbols. The sculpture of Rome and her Etruscan ancestors was designed to extol and to lead the dead into a world that was frightening but not unfathomable. It spoke of Man's divinity and justified his conquest of power, wealth and the world. It bade him cease bowing down before priests and stand erect; not as yet to deny God, but to look Him in the face.

*

The idiom of the Pisans and of artists like Cavallini, Arnolfo, Giotto, Tino di Camaino expressed the hopes of the Italian Ghibellines and the straining of the great municipalities towards independence. It also helped Pope Boniface VIII to proclaim the majesty of the Holy See and its mission to dominate the world as the Empire had done. Likewise it enabled the cardinals directing the vast constructions at Assisi to tame and discipline the Franciscan form of worship, transforming the Poverello into a champion of Roman supremacy. Yet this language was too unwonted and uncompromising. It was not wholly intelligible to the new men whom the flourishing Tuscan economy was introducing to the fine arts. It was completely alien to nations beyond the Alps. Moreover, the prestige of Gothic was still too influential; the Roman manner was unsuited to courtly conventions; the secularization of art was accompanied by a tendency for it to become more popular, which meant that it must use more commonplace, less disturbing means of expression. All these factors prevented the fourteenth-century Renaissance from adopting this idiom, so that the new art-forms emerging in Tuscany and Rome about 1300 acted merely as a ferment on French style, helping it to free itself more rapidly from Central Italy, whose vitality was soon undermined by the transfer of the papacy to Avignon, the decay of Pisa, the failures of imperial policy, the convulsions that wrought havoc among the great banking families of Florence and, finally, by the ravages of the plague. Nor did the stimulus affect Paris, where the Gothic tradition was too deeply rooted, but only a number of princely courts, which by their mode of chivalry were more receptive to Italian inspiration and could thus play a part in forwarding the new aesthetic movement.

The French court in Naples was the first to do so. Cavallini and Tino had worked there, and it may have been there that Simone Martini came to enrich his drawing with the new techniques of courtly imagination. Not long after, Pope Clement VI embarked at Avignon on the most ambitious undertaking of the century, in which Italian decorators collaborated with artists from the north of France. The papal court gave Matteo da Viterbo an even closer acquaintance with the fine points of chivalry than Simone Martini had acquired at Naples. About the middle of the century this painter achieved, with great facility, the first synthesis of the French and Tuscan manner. His work was exhibited in the main resort for all the princes and prelates of the world, who departed laden with *objets d'art* given to them by the Pope and his cardinals. The work of unification was thus begun by Matteo in Avignon, at the very center of Christendom and of the fourteenth century. Soon after there arose a magnificent patron in the Emperor Charles IV, heir to the Caesars but also, like his near relations the Valois Princes of France, wedded to Parisian taste. A lover of precious stones and bright ornament, he brought artists from Lombardy and the Rhineland to his court at Prague, where the Czech painters absorbed their teaching. Then, in the latter part of the century, the work of unification was taken up by the courts of Northern Italian "tyrants." These princes, who had usurped the sovereignty of the city republics, had close links with the court at Paris and were determined to be exemplars of chivalry and courtly elegance. Like the nobles north of the Alps, they were great horsemen, dog-fanciers and womanizers. Here the epics, romances and lyrical motifs imported from France flowered for the last time. But here, too, Giotto had painted, and Roman Italy was not far off. It was the painters employed by the lords of Milan and the patricians of Verona to illustrate their books who perfected the "Lombard style," uniting realism with the refinements of Gothic arabesque.

THE GREEK MODE

The frontier between the Greek and Latin provinces of the Roman Empire bisected the Italian peninsula, and during the earlier part of the Middle Ages the Emperors of Constantinople were bent on getting the whole of Italy into their hands. They proclaimed their might in Ravenna by the magnificence of their monuments, and Venice had long been subject to them. In the eighth century Rome and the South gave refuge to Byzantine monks who, persecuted by the Iconoclasts, brought with them their icons and illuminated manuscripts. Later, when merchants from the coastal towns of Italy ventured overseas they sought their fortunes in the Levant. At Byzantium and the cities of the Black Sea, even at Alexandria, they still encountered the Hellenic spirit. Finally, the Popes and the abbots of the great Italian monasteries constantly sought at Byzantium the craftsmen who could further their efforts to bring about an artistic revival. For all these reasons Italian art at the beginning of the fourteenth century was profoundly influenced by the Greek manner. This was true of all the decorative arts, painting especially.

The medium preferred was either mosaic or the illumination of small gilded panels intended to be placed side by side as in iconostases. Consequently one finds in Tuscan altarpieces that the story unfolds in a series of isolated episodes round the central hieratic figure of the Virgin or a Saint.

The Venetian-Byzantine tradition of craftsmanship was also faithfully observed when, about 1250, it was decided to clothe the vast interior of the baptistery at Florence in a gorgeous mantle of mosaic. This ubiquity of the Greek manner explains the astonishing way in which Duccio's scenes from the life of Christ, painted on the back of the Maestà which was borne triumphantly into the cathedral of Siena on June 9th, 1311, resemble frescoes painted a little earlier in Balkan monasteries, as well as contemporary mosaics in Byzantium.

THE DORMITION OF THE VIRGIN, ABOUT 1320. FRESCO, CHURCH OF GRACANICA (SERBIA).

DUCCIO (ABOUT 1260-1319). ALTARPIECE WITH THE MADONNA IN MAJESTY (MAESTÀ), 1308-1311. MUSEO DELL'OPERA DEL DUOMO, SIENA.

DUCCIO (ABOUT 1260-1319). SCENES FROM THE LIFE OF CHRIST ON THE BACK OF THE MAESTÀ, 1308-1311. MUSEO DELL'OPERA DEL DUOMO, SIENA.

THE DESCENT OF CHRIST INTO LIMBO, RIGHT SIDE: THE RESURRECTION OF EVE, 1310.
FRESCO IN THE PARECCLESION, CHURCH OF ST SAVIOUR IN THE CHORA (KAHRIEH DJAMI), ISTANBUL.

58

DUCCIO (ABOUT 1260-1319). THE THREE MARYS AT THE TOMB (DETAIL), 1308-1311.
PANEL ON THE BACK OF THE MAESTÀ. MUSEO DELL'OPERA DEL DUOMO, SIENA.

salvati aurea rutilatione resplenduit iuxta
quod psalmugraphus longe antea ipheïauit
Nox inquiens sicut dies illuminabitur et
sic facta est hec nox illuminatio mea ndelui
is meis dram subito michi dilectus filius afti
tit et refulgente inhabitaculo lumine hys
uerbis me dulciter salutauit. Aue inquit
mater mia aue. Quasi dicat ve iam merous
depone quia sine ue me inutero concepisti et
sine dolous molestia iurgo pmanens pepersti
plangere desine lacrimas absterge gemitus re
pelle suspiria reice Iam enim implete sut scrip
ture quia opoituit me pati et amortuus resur
gere Iam prostrato pncipe mortis infernum
erspoliaui potestatem nicelo et terra accepi et
ouem perditam adouile pro humero repor
taui quia hominem qui perierat ad regna
celestia reuocaui· Gaude igitur mater aman
tissima quia facta es celi et terre regina ···
Et sicut morte interueniente obtinui dominium
inferoium sic ascensionis gloria refulgente
regnum accipiam supernoix Ascendam igitur
ad patrem meum ut preparem me diligen
tibus locum Tu autem surge dilecta mea co
lumba mea speciosa mea electa michi ꝫ pre
electa incipe iam inpresenti gaudiu tibi infu
turo longe gloriosius eternaliter pmasura· Ulti
mo iummontem syon matre cu discipulis con

PASSIONAL OF ABBESS KUNIGUNDE: THE VIRGIN EMBRACING THE RESURRECTED CHRIST. PRAGUE, ABOUT 1320.
FOLIO 16 VERSO, MS XIV, A. 17, NATIONAL LIBRARY, PRAGUE.

60

2

THE LATIN INTONATION

When in the arts of Central Italy the Latin accent
again made itself heard, its return reflected a new
trend in political thought and practice. During the
twelfth century two powers struggled for the upper
hand in Europe: the Roman Empire, which Charlemagne had revived as a challenge to the emperors in
Constantinople, and the Roman Papacy, whose
primacy the Greek Church had refused to recognize
since 1054. Pope and Emperor were both eager to
find some legal sanction for their claim to power.
The professors of law at Bologna, whose business
it was to expound the Code of Justinian, were
accordingly invited to supply them with a clear
notion, supported by scholastic logic, of what
constituted the *imperium*—i.e. the legal right to
command and enforce the laws. Here was an issue
that at once evoked the glories of ancient Rome.
Henceforth the Hohenstaufens, who were kings of
Germany, and thereby "kings of the Romans" and
candidates for the Empire, vied with the Popes,
who were bishops and lords of Rome, for the
privilege of assuming the attributes of Caesar.
This competition, and the intellectual energies it
galvanized, gradually cleared the way for that
rediscovery of the Latin classics and the Roman
world which we call Humanism.

Thus were revealed not only texts and formulas
but a whole aesthetic which had once inspired the

monumental setting of the imperial *auctoritas*. The emperor Frederick II, heir of the Hohenstaufens but an Italian by birth, culture and sentiment, was thus led to revive, in Campania in the second third of the thirteenth century, the large-scale political sculpture of ancient Rome. The real starting point of Renaissance sculpture is to be found here, on the confines of the Eastern Empire, of which Southern Italy had hitherto been one of the outlying provinces. It was not until 1260 however, in the Baptistery of Pisa, that Latin forms of expression impinged decisively on the style of religious art. The Western Empire had fallen apart after the death of Frederick II (1250). The Kingdom of Sicily, which Frederick had inherited from his mother, passed a few years later into the hands of a French prince, Charles of Anjou, brother of St Louis, and soon the graceful forms of Gothic art were being imported into Naples. The imperial spirit of enterprise, the sense of fidelity to the Roman past—these took root not in the South but in Central Italy, particularly at Pisa on the Tuscan coast.

Pisa had been enriched by trade with the Levant, and a large part of her wealth went to erect the splendid group of buildings—cathedral, baptistery, campanile and Campo Santo—which proclaimed the glory of the city. Lying on the main road by which the German kings traveled to Rome, Pisa gave them their first taste of a world where something of the grandeur of Roman antiquity lingered on. Pisa moreover was a Ghibelline stronghold, loyal to the Empire, cherishing the memory of Frederick II, eager to emulate the majestic monuments commissioned by Frederick at Capua. Nicola Pisano, a South Italian by birth, was schooled in the techniques of Campanian sculpture; he saw and studied the figure carvings on Late Antique sarcophagi; he made of St Peter a Roman hero, of the Virgin a Roman matron; he created the new style of Renaissance sculpture.

But Pisa, her fleet shattered by the Genoese, was on the decline. The overland trade route between Latium and the plain of the Po shifted from Pisa to Florence, and economic power passed into the hands of the Florentines. They too felt themselves to be ancient Romans at heart. About 1300 Nicola's son Giovanni Pisano, with his pupils Arnolfo di Cambio and Tino di Camaino, produced in the Roman spirit, at Pisa, Florence and Siena, the first pieces of large-scale sculpture which, since the decline of Romanesque statuary, could vie with the Gothic sculpture of the Ile-de-France. They have a rugged strength and majesty which the latter lacks: the Virgins of the Tuscan sculptors seem to be carrying not only the Christ Child but the weight of the world. Unlike the French cathedral sculptors, the Tuscans sought to convey an inner torment, the pathos of the Franciscan preachers. Their sensitive carving re-echoes at times the dramatic accent of Cimabue's great *Crucifixion* at Assisi; it recaptures the surging movement of the hunting scenes and renderings of such themes as the Crossing of the Red Sea carved on the sides of Late Byzantine sarcophagi.

Their success in the struggle against the emperors impelled the popes to adopt an imperial policy of their own. They called on the new school of Tuscan art to give tangible expression to their power and prestige for the benefit of pilgrims to the Holy City. As the Jubilee of 1300 approached, Rome saw an unprecedented concourse of architects and artists. It was now that, following that of sculpture, the language of painting, which had hitherto been Greek (i.e. Byzantine), was translated into Latin. In his mosaics at Santa Maria in Trastevere in 1291, then in his Santa Cecilia frescoes, Cavallini created a whole series of solid, majestic figures. It was Giotto, however, who led the movement to break away from the stereotyped forms of Byzantine art. Heir of the Tuscan sculptors, he painted some figures in grisaille which have all the plastic qualities of statuary. In his frescoes he went even further in the naturalistic delineation of man and the world. Thanks to Giotto, painting became the major art form of Europe, and has remained so during the six centuries since his death.

At Avignon the Pope and most of the cardinals were Frenchmen from the Midi imbued with Gothic taste and the code of chivalry. Nevertheless, for the decoration of the palace which the Pope had just built to the glory of a second Rome, he commissioned a Sienese, Simone Martini, the most famous painter of the day. Simone had in fact been working for some time for the Angevin princes of Naples, for whom he had adapted the Tuscan style to suit the aristocratic languor and grace, as well as the affectation, of French taste. At Avignon, virtually nothing remains of the frescoes for which he was responsible; but his cartoons, or working drawings, traced out in Sinope red on the preparatory coat of plaster, have recently come to light on the walls of the Palace of the Popes. At the west end of the cathedral of Notre-Dame-des-Doms the artist made several sketches of Christ in Glory, with the Virgin seated on the ground "in all humility." They well reveal the elegance, strength of line and rhythmic power of his composition. The Ambrosian Library in Milan possesses a Virgil illustrated by Simone while at the papal court. One wonders whether the artist's adaptation of his pictures to the classical text was spontaneous or dictated by the humanist who ordered the work. No other painting of the Trecento is more akin to the ancients, either in conception or in the visual techniques employed.

Simone died in 1344. The bulk of the prodigious plan for decorating the court at Avignon was carried out between 1343 and 1368 by another Italian, Matteo Giovannetti da Viterbo, and his assistants. By this time creative artists were beginning to feel the lack of real stimulus which Central Italy, impoverished by financial crises and the exile of the papacy, could no longer provide. Meanwhile, Matteo found in the Rhone valley the first burgeoning of French art. The Pope and his cardinals, with a suspicious eye on the waywardness of Franciscan mysticism, welcomed the ostentation, finery and courtly manners that came from Paris. They allowed their artist complete freedom of invention, with the result that he merged Gothic lyricism with the broad spaciousness of the Tuscan School.

At the very time when Matteo and his assistants were at work in Avignon, Charles IV was seeking to restore the Empire and to build in Bohemia a capital worthy of its greatness. He founded the University of Prague in 1348, its organization being modeled on that of the University of Paris (where Charles had himself been a student) ; and he attracted to his court a host of architects, painters and sculptors, many of them from France. It was Mathieu d'Arras who designed the cathedral of St Vitus, whose pillared apse evoked the woodland groves of knightly romance. Descended from the Counts of Luxembourg, the Emperor was closely related to the royal house of France, and court life in Prague took its cue from Paris. From the court of Bohemia the refinements of Gothic art were diffused through Central Europe. Charles IV, however, was well aware of the dual character, at once Germanic and Roman, of the ancient empire over which he ruled ; he had been crowned emperor in Rome and he realized that in Italy lay one of the sources of his power. It was only natural therefore that he should commission an Italian artist, Tommaso da Modena, to paint the altarpiece for the upper chapel at Karlstein. It was probably Nicolas Wurmser, a master from Strasbourg, who carried out the frescoes nearby, notably one in which the Emperor is seen as the servant of God, stooping over the reliquaries of the Passion. Thus the graceful style of the Ile-de-France, the Gothic traditions of the Rhineland and the plastic innovations of Northern Italy converged upon Prague from the opposite ends of the Empire ; but the genius loci was wholly Czech and proved wonderfully rich in creative energy.

For at least a century past Bohemia had ceased to be a land of peasants and woodsmen ; it had prospered, Prague had become the center of a vast network of trade relations, and wealthy princes and churchmen were surrounding themselves with precious objects and works of art commissioned from local artists and craftsmen. Throughout the four- teenth century prayer books were being illustrated with admirable miniatures, such as those in the Passional of Abbess Kunigunde which, however, still owe much to French models imported into Bohemia. Panel painters were active too. As early as 1350 the anonymous author of the Vysebrod Cycle had not only adopted and made his own the latest discoveries of Tuscan art, but had lent an added nobility to the narrative style of French stained-glass. By far the most striking products of Prague's golden age are the figures painted by the Bohemian, Master Theodoric, on the niches where relics were kept in the chapel at Karlstein. The features of his saints have a full-blooded eloquence far removed from the weak and willowy Gothic manner. This individuality was soon to be recaptured by the unidentified artist who painted the portrait of Rudolph IV of Hapsburg in the Diocesan Museum at Vienna.

SIMONE MARTINI (ABOUT 1285-1344). FRONTISPIECE OF PETRARCH'S "VIRGIL," ABOUT 1340.
MS A 79 INF., BIBLIOTECA AMBROSIANA, MILAN.

MATTEO GIOVANNETTI DA VITERBO (MID-14TH CENTURY). THE VISION OF ST JOHN AT PATMOS (DETAIL), 1346-1348.
FRESCO IN THE CHAPEL OF ST JOHN, PALACE OF THE POPES, AVIGNON.

MASTER THEODORIC OF PRAGUE (ACTIVE 1348-1367). ST JEROME. PANEL PAINTING FROM THE CASTLE OF KARLSTEIN.
NATIONAL GALLERY, PRAGUE.

NICOLAS WURMSER (ACTIVE MID-14TH CENTURY). THE EMPEROR CHARLES IV PLACING RELICS IN THE SHRINE OF THE CHAPEL
OF THE HOLY CROSS, BEFORE 1357. FRESCO IN THE LADY CHAPEL, CASTLE OF KARLSTEIN, NEAR PRAGUE.

MASTER OF VYSEBROD (ACTIVE MID-14TH CENTURY). THE RESURRECTION, ABOUT 1350.
NATIONAL GALLERY, PRAGUE.

THE MISZLE VIRGIN AND CHILD, ABOUT 1330. POLYCHROME WOOD. NATIONAL GALLERY, PRAGUE.

THE TWO PATHS

It was about 1400 that the artistic developments which throughout the Trecento had been gaining ground in the entourage of the great princes of Europe found in Paris the ideal conditions for their completion and widest dissemination. From Paris the resulting synthesis of styles spread to all the aristocracy of the West—an aristocracy which, continually thrown together by their common pleasures and tournaments, their summer crusades in Prussia and incessant campaigning from one province to another, had been moulded into a homogeneous class, sharing the same parlance and outlook, the same ways and tastes. The long wars with England had come to an end, for the time being, and the advantage lay with the King of France. He stood now on a stronger footing; and, most important of all, he had grown richer, for the system of taxation wrought out in the stress of war was bringing into his coffers an abundant supply of gold which he could spend as he pleased. After the death of Charles IV the Empire had relapsed into impotence. The Papacy was divided against itself, with rival popes in Rome and Avignon. The hegemony of Europe thus fell to the King of France and to the sister courts of his uncles, the Dukes of Anjou, Berry and Burgundy. The sumptuous commissions of these princes caused artists from many parts of Europe to flock to Bourges and Angers, to Mehun-sur-Yèvre and the Chartreuse de Champmol at Dijon, but above all to Paris. Here the Lombard masters introduced the modernisms of illusionist painting, that concrete, sharply focused vision of the world which we find in the Veronese miniatures illustrating the *Tacuinum Sanitatis*. They introduced the techniques of *trompe-l'œil* to all the artists who came from the Netherlands in the wake of the sculptors of funerary effigies. These artists took them up and applied them less accurately but with a more vigorous and forthright touch, though rough and even uncouth at times. The art currents of North and South converged in Paris, mingling there with the elegance of the Gothic tradition; and thanks to the thriving trade in works of art, to their diffusion in the shape of gifts from one prince to another, and to the prestige of the royal court in Paris, the forms born of this union spread all over Europe.

Throughout this activity, and especially the synthesis in which it culminated, the prevailing mode of expression was French. This was only natural, for the secular power that dominated fourteenth-century culture was not Roman but chivalrous; and chivalry was French by origin and in its idiom, whether in Cyprus, Pampeluna or Windsor—or, for that matter, in Florence. The language that subjugated Europe in 1400, even including Tuscany, was therefore essentially Gothic. Artificial, two-dimensional, indifferent to the meaning of weight, mass and empty space, it had hardly accepted anything of the Roman renaissance, apart from a few of the techniques of realism. Patrons did not want their artists to produce monuments of stoic grandeur, but to portray the pleasure of living. In other words, they wanted reality to be translated into dreams and sport, in exactly the same way as society had long since adopted the make-believe of prowess and courtliness. Their requirements were met by an increasing resort to arabesque and *trompe-l'œil*. These two devices led to the fullest expression of courtliness in fourteenth-century art and, at the same time, severed its links with the divine and brought it down to the level of man. This is the heart of the matter. The new form of art, even when fulfilling a religious purpose, no longer spoke to priests but to men. When Giotto related the life of Christ, he presented it as a play, set on a stage with symbolic scenery. The world he portrays in his masque is not supernatural or liturgical but human. It tells a factual, human story, the tragedy of the man Jesus and the woman Mary. The other characters, on a par with them, are real men whom only the dignity of their bearing raises to the height of the living God. In a heroic, Roman manner Giotto has expressed what is, perhaps, the essence of the Franciscan spirit: the striving by Man to live like Jesus, like a god, like God Himself. A hundred years later, in the emotional technique employed by the Master of the Rohan Hours to depict "in the Gothic manner" the agony of Christ crucified, one finds the humanizing of divine figures carried to the opposite extreme. In both cases fourteenth-century art represents God and Man as brothers.

A mystic like Tauler believed that men could, through humility, come so near to God that they became "godly men." Such nearness to a God made flesh in the beliefs and sufferings of His creatures clearly put an end to many proscriptions, such as the Church's denunciation of human virtues and delights. The new men, freed from the priests, felt the urge both to commune more deeply with Christ and to enjoy the world. In daily life the twin courses of mysticism and naturalism, first charted by William of Occam, led to a double standard of behavior. Prince Louis d'Orléans and Queen Elizabeth of Bavaria "did all the pleasures prove." Yet he would make occasional retreats to a monastery, where he would hear five masses a day in his cell; while she had a meditation on the Passion of Jesus composed for her daily orisons. Karlstein, the fairy-tale castle built by Charles IV, opens onto the forests of Bohemia through courtyards designed for jousting and the meets of his hunt; but it also leads, by a plan that faithfully echoes the stages of mystical illumination, to a Sainte-Chapelle built for communion with the relics of Golgotha. The Lazarus with the body of Apollo, whom the Limbourg brothers caused to rise from the dead, displays to Jesus, his friend, the glory of his physical beauty. In art as in life, men divided their joy between imitating Christ and possessing the world.

The courtiers of Paris and Nicosia, of Windsor and Naples, danced on the rim of a volcano which they called Hell. They lived in a whirl of gaiety. They wore cloth of gold and rode blood stallions and made love to long-limbed girls. Yet they trembled in the knowledge that the life they clung to so eagerly was beset by darkness and horror and the threat of countless evils—plague, pain, the madness that turned kings into beasts, death and the unknown that lay beyond. Hag-ridden by their peril, they were driven to the extremes of asceticism or pleasure. The rather mawkish charm of early fifteenth-century art cannot quite conceal the black despair which causes the executioner to grin so horribly in scenes of martyrdom, or the Three Marys to wring their hands as they see the wounds of Christ. It is that despair which, at Barcelona, caused Bernardo Martorell to quicken the sense of pain and tragedy by lengthening out the body of the martyred St George along a tense diagonal. Princes in their anguish were obsessed by the Apocalypse, which revealed to them the flaws of creation.

After 1373 Nicolas Bataille, the most famous of Parisian weavers, was working for Louis, Duc d'Anjou, on his amazing portrayal in tapestry of the Revelation of St John the Divine. In this case the subject is rendered less disturbing by elegant draftsmanship and perfect harmony of colors. The Beast of the Apocalypse becomes part of the harmless ritual of chivalry, along with unicorns, gallant Hector and doughty Charlemagne.

Some years earlier, however, on the walls of the lady-chapel at Karlstein, an unknown hand had painted blind terror, the end of all things, the great spider and livid faces that come wheeling in a nightmare. Pisanello's St George, in the church of Sant' Anastasia at Verona, is no slayer of dragons, nor are his eyes on the princess. Is he not rather waking, dazed, from some hideous dream, against that background of storm, gallows and icing-sugar architecture?

NICOLAS BATAILLE (ACTIVE 2ND HALF OF 14TH CENTURY). THE ANGERS APOCALYPSE: "THE GREAT WHORE THAT SITTETH UPON MANY WATERS" (REVELATION, XVII, I). DETAIL OF THE TAPESTRY OF THE APOCALYPSE, 1373-1380. MUSÉE DES TAPISSERIES, ANGERS.

ANTONIO PISANELLO (1395-ABOUT 1455). THE LEGEND OF ST GEORGE AND THE PRINCESS (DETAIL), ABOUT 1435.
FRESCO, CHURCH OF SANT'ANASTASIA, VERONA.

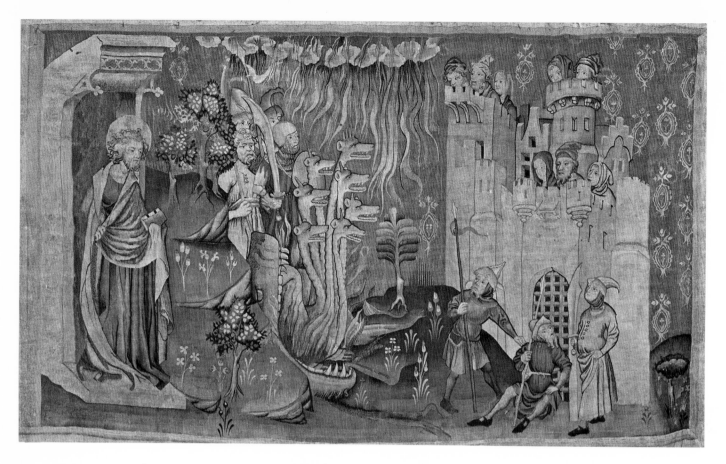

NICOLAS BATAILLE (ACTIVE 2ND HALF OF 14TH CENTURY). THE ANGERS APOCALYPSE: THE ASSAULT ON THE CITY OF GOD BY THE HOSTS OF GOG AND MAGOG AT THE INSTANCE OF SATAN (REVELATION, XX, 7-9). DETAIL OF THE TAPESTRY OF THE APOCALYPSE, 1373-1380. MUSÉE DES TAPISSERIES, ANGERS.

MASTER OF THE APOCALYPSE. THE DESTRUCTION OF THE CITY, ABOUT 1370. FRESCO IN THE LADY CHAPEL, CASTLE OF KARLSTEIN, NEAR PRAGUE.

THE TRIUMPH OF DEATH

The fresco of the Triumph of Death *was designed for that most noble of cemeteries, the Campo Santo at Pisa, where it was accompanied by two others, depicting the Last Judgement and the exemplary life of the anchorites in the Thebaid. Like them, it was a summons to repentance and self-denial; but it also cried out to believers with a new accent of despair. The unknown artist had, in fact, exploited all the means of visual exhortation whereby the Mendicant Orders sought to edify the masses. It was the wealthy who stood in the direst peril, and they above all must be indoctrinated, weaned from fleshly delights and compelled to die in the faith. Two pictures were used, like successive arguments in a sermon, to drive the point home. In a leafy glade where knights and ladies were riding amid the flowers and the animals they knew so well, the artist set out the hackneyed parable of the Three Dead and the Three Living, with the sudden discovery of a corpse rotting in the sunlight. This well-worn theme, however, was greatly intensified by the adjoining picture, unprecedented in those days, of Death Triumphant, swiftly mowing down those who dallied in the garden of Love.*

The worldly-wise could not avoid the moral impact of such a vision. By dwelling on the beauties of this world—soft grass, rich dresses and sweet airs—the painter played upon man's dread of losing them. He took the tasteful designs with which Parisian craftsmen adorned the ivory toilet requisites of fashionable women and, with a turn of the screw, placed them on the walls of a graveyard. Over the main doorway of Leon Cathedral an earlier generation of sculptors had used a very similar gathering of courtly singers and musicians to exemplify the raptures of paradise; whereas the group at Pisa represent the guilty pleasures of this world, which man should renounce. He who relishes them sees in Death, Medicina di ogni pena, *the terrifying power that will snatch them away.*

The new teaching no longer offers men a gentle transition to assured, unearthly bliss. It is rooted in hard reality and the unconquerable fact of death. Knightly pleasures are extolled only that men shall be more aware of the final tragedy. Their faith must be nourished by consciousness of their own bleak destiny.

THE TRIUMPH OF DEATH, ABOUT 135⦁

FRESCO IN THE CAMPO SANTO, PISA.

II

IMITATION OF CHRIST

THE LAYMAN'S CHRISTIANITY

The modernist tendency of the fourteenth century consisted very largely in a change of religious outlook and in "modern" forms of worship which were the result of the great conversion from medieval Christianity. By a very long process, beginning with the first mutterings of heresy in the eleventh century and reaching a sudden climax after 1200 with the preaching of St Francis of Assisi, the Christian religion had ceased to be ritual and sacerdotal. By the fourteenth century it had become the faith of the masses and priestly authority had been weakened. This age was no less Christian on that account than its predecessor; on the contrary, it was undoubtedly more so, for its faith was more personal, broader in scope and more firmly rooted in the Gospel. Hitherto the Christian life, to which Europe paid lip service, had only been lived fully by a small élite. As a result of this transformation Christianity became the religion of the people.

It also became more naïve. By assuming the homespun of a popular creed it was to some extent insured against doubt; for among the newly converted masses there was more credulousness and zealotry, a more benighted acceptance of the supernatural than there had been in cloister, chapter-house or quadrangle. The simple, fourteenth-century Christian was less exposed to the snares of unbelief; but he also went in greater terror of the Beyond, of those fearful powers, mysterious yet apparent, whom he must propitiate throughout life and especially at the dread moment of leaving it. The religion of the great thirteenth-century prelates, having overcome such terrors, developed in tranquillity, hopefulness and light; but the popular religion, which the Church accepted and tried to discipline, was a prey to darkness and fear of the occult. There emerged once more the demons which Gothic sunlight had driven into the darkest corners of cathedrals and which had hidden away in heretical sects or among magic springs and elf-haunted forests. Fourteenth-century laymen went in fear

of them, as of the pantocrator, and their religious life revolved round the daily act of pious prophylaxis which sought to exorcise the powers of evil and earn the compassion of God. In the new Christianity the layman was no longer, like his forefathers, the mute, uncomprehending spectator of liturgical rites; he now practised his religion according to his lights. This was true of rulers like Elizabeth of Bavaria, of Thuringian robber-knights, of scholarly women like Christine de Pisan and her fellow-countrymen, the Italian bankers, of Hanseatic merchants and wealthy farmers, down to the humble village hind. The work of art was one of the means whereby this practice found expression, whether it was a work of praise and fervor or of sacrifice and dedication of wealth; whether it was propitiatory or intended to prompt divine intervention. In every way it had come more than ever to fulfil a religious purpose.

The great change, however, was that art now obeyed the longings of the laity. Apart from all the economic and social changes that have been briefly examined, the relationship of the priest to his flock had been transformed. For centuries the Western Church had acted as a spiritual clearing-house. The clergy, both secular and monastic, prayed for the laity who supplied them with gifts, and their prayers obtained grace which was distributed among the faithful. By his alms and in accordance with a fixed tariff, every believer secured a portion of grace for himself and his family. This was expected to counterbalance his sins at the Last Judgement. On the threshold of great churches the image of St Michael weighing souls stood as a reminder of the redemptive power of this transaction. For the salvation of all, the clergy erected monuments of sacred art that were truly communal.

The disturbing successes of heresy, whereby a more educated laity sought release from its passive role and compensation for its repressions, led the

Church in the thirteenth century to renew its pastoral vocation. It could not depend upon the parish priests, ill-educated and often badly selected, who in any case tended more and more to live away from their cures and draw their stipend *in absentia*. Nor could it rely on the very humble men who actually did the work. It was the Mendicant Orders who, in the towns at least, took the lead and for this purpose developed methods of organizing and inspiring the masses.

With a view to co-ordinating the laity in a more dynamic body than the parish, the Friars Minor and Predicant enrolled among their Tertiaries all those who, without taking the tonsure, wanted no longer to see their faith through a glass darkly, but to live it. Many of these men had either embraced heresy or would have been constrained to do so. The less devout should at least unite in fraternities and guilds, in those associations for mutual benefit and occasional dissipation which the Church had long condemned for harboring pagan superstitions, but which in the fourteenth century it began to encourage, supervise and control. Grouped round an oracle, such as the image of a patron saint, endowed by the contributions of their members, these brotherhoods proliferated. There were craft, district and parish brotherhoods, hospital societies and charities, groups of penitents whose members ceremonially flogged one another, groups of worship, like the Italian *laudesi*, seeking to die in the odor of sanctity, whose main work consisted in edifying their members by "laudes," a form of community singing, and by staging, sometimes with considerable skill, scenes from the Gospel, such as the Nativity or the Road to Calvary. The Third Orders and the innumerable brotherhoods offered their members, who comprised the vast majority of town-dwelling laymen and a good many of those in the country, a spiritual life based on monastic practice: withdrawal into the cloister of silent prayer, the heroic struggle to win through to salvation, fasting, abstinence and daily spiritual exercises such as the chanting of psalms and recitation of canonical hours. The new administration bade the laity pray spontaneously, utter the words of Holy Writ and, if they could do so, read, mark, learn and inwardly digest them. It made the liturgy of convent and cathedral accessible to ordinary men and women in their everyday lives and in the privacy of their hearts.

In order that the people should receive instruction and the activities of the brotherhoods bear fruit, the missionaries of the Mendicant Orders fully exploited such means of edification as the pulpit and the stage, which were used in conjunction. When St Francis realized that it was not enough to attain his own salvation and that Christ commissioned him to broadcast His message, he did so by the spoken word. He was not a priest; so he sang of penitence, perfect joy and the love of God as a minstrel might have done, and the world heard him. Then he sent his disciples out along the roads and into workshops to use the same, very simple methods of persuasion. St Dominic founded his Rule for preaching. In order that the exponents of heresy, who lived with the people and spoke their language, might be beaten on their own ground, the Dominican intellectuals took the traditional homily of cathedrals and monasteries, which had only been addressed to churchmen, and made it a most effective weapon of propaganda. For this purpose they transposed the devout discourse of learned rhetoric into common speech and brought its argument down to the level of the least sophisticated audience. In the thirteenth century the sermon, like the prayer book, emerged from the cloisters and enclosed communities and was diffused among the people. After 1300 popular preaching gained steadily in influence.

The 1380's saw the beginning of the great missions and the campaigns of itinerant preachers. The fame of their mystical feats went before them and at the city gates they would be awaited by the whole municipality. Soon the squares would fill with listeners in a frenzy of enthusiasm. The crowd expected them to work miracles, dispel pestilence and, above all, show the way to a new life in this world and salvation hereafter. Of the Franciscan, Brother Richard, who preached at Paris in 1429, it is recorded that "he began his sermon about five in the morning. It lasted until ten or eleven and was heard every day by five or six thousand people. With his back to the charnel-house and facing the Charonnerie, the site of the Danse Macabre, he preached from a platform about a yard and a half high. The people of Paris were so moved to godliness that within three or four hours you could have seen more than a hundred bonfires, where they were burning gaming tables, backgammon boards, dice, playing cards, billiard balls and cues, in fact every sort of game that rouses men to anger and causes them to curse and swear like gamblers. That day and the next, women would burn their finery and maidens would sacrifice their peaked headdresses, their trains and all manner of fripperies." These agitators often stooped to catchpenny methods and sob-stuff. By reaching down into men's hearts they hoped to tap the deepest springs of emotion and thereby achieve mass-conversions. Wyclif denounced such ignoble tactics, and Chaucer's Pardoner is an evil charlatan. Yet their inexhaustible eloquence revealed and imparted to the people a brotherly, deeply moving image of Christ. It was the more convincing because their sermons were accompanied by a genuinely popular and festive show, which provided a setting of graphic paintings and sculptures, processions of singers and dramatic performances.

The theater, of course, originated in liturgy and as early as the tenth century was used to bring it within reach of the people. Like preaching, however, whose success it shared, it only became really popular and widespread in the fourteenth century. On the two great feasts of Christendom, Easter and Christmas, and on those of patron saints, the Italian brotherhoods performed countless *sacre rappresentazioni*. These were *tableaux vivants* which gradually became part of processions, were arranged in a series of scenes and acquired action, dialogue, music and fixed scenery. They were really private performances, reserved exclusively to members of a religious association whom they were intended to edify. But they acquired a deeper significance, for by miming the sufferings of Christ men could better comprehend the Passion and identify themselves with Him. By the end of the century, when the first great preaching missions were beginning, the theater had widened its scope and achieved its aim of becoming a huge, communal celebration. In Paris, London and other big towns the brotherhoods excelled in annual public performances of the Passion. Thus began the fifty most fertile years in the history of European religious drama.

The scene-shifting and make-believe, the chanting flagellants, the words and gesticulations from the pulpit were addressed not to the intellect but to the emotions. Their aim was to induce salutary feelings of pity and fear in every spectator. Whether in the midst of his fraternity or in the congregation at a sermon or in the audience at a mystery-play, each man felt himself involved. His soul and salvation were at stake; his responsibility and guilt were in the scales; the bell tolled for him. Deeply implanted in the emotions and quickened by the fear of God, this was a more disturbing, far more private Christianity. It took the form of dialogue: a dialogue between the penitent and his confessor in the secrecy of contrition, the whispered avowal of misconduct and absolution; a dialogue between the soul and God. By preaching and play-acting, by all the manœuvres of a direct approach, the Mendicant Orders stole converts from their rival, the secular Church. They also took over the anti-clerical tendencies of the heretical sects which they had originally been commissioned to lead back to the fold, and whose revival was now impeded by their activities.

All these movements swept through fourteenth-century Christianity and multiplied, sometimes to a dangerous extent. On the southern flanks of Europe, in Provence and Italy, where the Catharian and Waldensian heresies still exerted a strong residual influence, an entire branch of the Franciscan Order plunged into violent opposition to the Avignonese papacy. In claiming to be "spirituals," these "Little Brothers" were only showing devotion to their Founder; but they also expressed belief, founded on the works of the Calabrian hermit, Joachim of Floris, in the advent of a Third Age. After those of the Father and the Son, the teaching of St Francis had ushered in the Age of the Holy Ghost, in whose kingdom the intercession of the Church was no longer needed, since all true believers were filled with the Spirit, which the Roman Church was in fact betraying. These beliefs were echoed by the Rhenish communities of Beghards and Brothers of the Free Spirit. In 1326 they were hunted down and burned by the episcopacy because they, likewise, proclaimed the absolute freedom of the *perfecti* and the identification of the soul with God in mystic communion: "Feeling and possessing a natural state of inward peace, they believe themselves to be free and at rest, united to God without need of mediation, exalted above all the rites of the holy Church, above the commandments of God and above the law." Strange echoes of this pernicious doctrine could be heard in the Dominican convents where Meister Eckhart was teaching. In one of his sermons delivered in the vernacular he said: "Verily the power of the Holy Spirit takes what is most pure, delicate and sublime, the spark of the soul, and carries it up into the bright blaze of Love. So it is with a tree, when the sun takes what is purest and most sublime in its roots and carries it up to the branches where it becomes blossom. In the same way the spark of the soul is borne aloft to the light of the Holy Spirit and thus returns to its source. It becomes wholly one with God, so completely at one that it is more truly a part of God than food is of the body."

Later, at the end of the century, opposition to the hierarchy assumed harsher, more uncompromising forms in England and Bohemia. In the eyes of Wyclif, of the Lollard preachers and of the knights who heard them, the corrupt clergy were useless. The essence of religious life was to adore Christ the Brother and read the Gospel. The Word of God must therefore be translated into the common tongue, so that the people might hear it. These ideas were followed up by John Huss, who released the deepest springs of popular messianism. Briefly, before the outbreak of violence and slaughter, it succeeded in creating on a symbolic Mount Tabor an egalitarian family of the children of God, filled with the Holy Spirit and eagerly awaiting the imminent end of time. It was, however, in the Netherlands and in a far more restrained and submissive manner that the movement calmly attained its fullest expression by initiating what was rightly known as "modern worship." For some time laymen, priests and Dominicans had been founding on the Rhine little groups of "friends of God," who helped one another to adopt a rule of Christian brotherliness that should forsake the world and lead them to enlightenment. In his *Zierde der geistlichen Hochzeit* Ruysbroek urged his communities to practise complete self-denial in order to achieve union in Jesus. "A man who truly lives within himself suffices unto himself. He is freed from earthly cares and his heart opens reverently to the eternal goodness of God. Then the heavens are revealed and from the face of divine love a sudden light pierces his open heart like a thunderbolt. In that light the voice of God speaks to the loving heart: 'I am thine and thou art mine. I dwell in thee and thou in Me.' " In the Brotherhood of Common Life, founded by Gerhard Groot after he had long hesitated between the anchoretic life of Ruysbroek and the asceticism of the Carthusians, there was written before 1424 the devotional work which has enjoyed the most enduring success among the Christian laymen, the *Imitation of Christ*.

The priest still had a part to play in an act of meditation that did not attempt to fathom the mystery of God but to encounter Christ in His Humanity and gradually to blend with Him in inexpressible union. Since Jesus is nowhere more accessible than at the Lord's Supper, certain rites could not be dispensed with. The priestly office was rendered necessary by the essential meaning of the Mass, as a reconstruction of the Passion, at which men hoped to see, as long ago at Bolsena, blood ooze from the wafer or the figure of the Man of Sorrows rise from the chalice; or of the solemn, winding procession of Corpus Christi, when the body of Christ was displayed. Yet what mattered above all was "inward and spiritual grace," prayer, adoration by the soul and the gradual exaltation of its "ground." It was from these that the new forms of religious art took their fullest meaning.

THE CHAPEL

Fourteenth-century Christendom built many noble places of public worship. In those parts of Europe, such as England or Spain, where the landed gentry were still wealthy, abbots and canons sometimes renovated their churches. Elsewhere, religious houses received subsidies from a bishop, a patron or, as in the South of France, a Pope. In the case of monasteries, cathedrals and churches whose function was unchanged, there was no attempt at structural alteration. Innovations consisted either in some ornamental feature, an embellishment to the glory of its donor, or in enclosing the sanctuary by means of a rood-screen. That in the Capilla Mayor at Toledo forms a gorgeous but impenetrable barrier, enabling the celebrants to intone their office in seclusion and completely shutting out the congregation. Thus the final development of hieratic art emphasized the separation of liturgical tradition from the people.

Municipalities, meanwhile, were building churches for their townsfolk. They sought to glorify their city by erecting great parochial buildings, relegating the local tabernacles to the role of chapels-of-ease. These parish churches were intended to assemble the citizens, guilds and authorities in municipal ceremonies that were civic as much as religious. The big collegiate churches in Flanders, St Mary Radcliffe in Bristol, or Tinn, the merchants' church in Prague, could hold their own with cathedrals. They were proud and self-assertive, symbolizing power by means of lofty naves and steeples. Not far away another type of church was appearing, more spiritual in purpose and better suited to the new evangelical movement. These were the churches built by the four Mendicant Orders on the outskirts of every big town. The Austin friars, the grey Franciscans, the black Dominicans and the white Carmelites were all constructing immense halls for the new mode of worship, often designed with two naves, one for the Brothers and the other thrown open to the laity.

These churches exemplified self-denial, to which the Orders of poverty were beholden. Outside there were no buttresses but a severely plain, homogeneous mass, adapted in all respects to its function and on that account of great beauty. Within there was the same simplicity and unity. There might be several naves, but they were all the same height, for religious and laity are equal before God. They were only separated by a few slender pillars, with the aim of uniting in one body the people and the friars who led them. To ensure full participation by the laity, the new design was the absolute antithesis of the rood-screen. Everyone in the church must be able to hear the preacher, see the elevation of the Host, and even read a book. More glass was used, bays were widened and the gloom appropriate to tapers and chanting was dispelled. The Mendicants' design, huge, bare, sober, light and airy, soon to be adopted by collegiate churches and even cathedrals, provided a perfect auditorium for the spectacle that the public expression of piety had now become. Along the walls were placed rows of side-chapels for the private devotions of families and brotherhoods.

Originally the chapel had been regarded as an appurtenance of royalty, belonging to a sovereign endowed with charismatic and thaumaturgical powers. According to the ancient German belief, which lies at the root of the European concept of monarchy, the king held converse with the gods, officiated for his people and by his intercession secured victory and prosperity for them. In Carolingian times the ceremony of consecration christianized this magic office and brought it within the province of the Church. The sovereign was thus, like a bishop, the anointed of God. He had lost none of his religious attributes, but now he held them direct from God, whom he represented on earth in the conduct of temporal business. He was now responsible for the spiritual welfare of his people and bore witness of it before God. It was part of his calling that he always stood in immediate and personal relationship to the divine power. The king was the first layman, for a long time the only one, to pray as a priest. This accounts for the touching fervor with which Charlemagne spent sleepless nights wrestling with the alphabet. The royal household now comprised a staff of chaplains whose duty it was to encompass the monarch, like a bishop in his cathedral, with an uninterrupted act of worship. Its setting was the chapel, where the king had his throne, his episcopal *cathedra*. He was surrounded by his lieges and before him were displayed the holy relics of his treasury; for it behoved the sovereign, in order to enhance his powers of intercession, to collect as many fragments as possible of the saintliest bodies. The chapel was also, perhaps primarily, a reliquary: both a shrine and a monstrance for holy remains. The walls were lined with the most costly materials to provide a magnificent setting both for the relics and for the sovereign himself as he sat throned in majesty, bearing the symbols of his authority. Such was the chapel built by Charlemagne, on the lines of the oratories of the Eastern Roman Empire, for his palace at Aix-la-Chapelle. Such, too, was the Sainte-Chapelle in Paris, the supreme masterpiece of royal liturgical art, constructed by St Louis as a receptacle for the Crown of Thorns.

Throughout the fourteenth century European monarchs imitated this perfect example. Edward III of England, as soon as he had wrested power from his mother, determined to assert his youthful daring and vigor by proving himself equal to the King of France. At Westminster, close to the tomb of Edward the Confessor, whom he caused to be honored as a rival to St Louis, he built a chapel dedicated to St Stephen. When Charles IV of Bohemia sought to bring renewed lustre to the imperial diadem he had received, he constructed Karlstein. At the summit of this fairy-tale castle he placed a shrine inlaid with gold and bright jewels, its walls adorned with portraits of saints. This reliquary for the True Cross was, as it were, the mystical climax of the warlike and chivalrous virtues displayed in the lower courtyards. A long, heavenward ascent led to the chapel with its hidden precinct, jealously guarded by a series of ramparts and fragrant with the odor of sanctity, where the Emperor would be closeted with the crucified God whose Vicar on earth he felt himself to be.

Kings, however, were not the only men to build themselves sanctuaries in the fourteenth century, for unanointed princes also wanted to have theirs. A wonderful example is that at Bourges, where the Duc Jean de Berry placed the religious objects in his gorgeous collection of jewels. But the new trend in pious observances and the general dissemination of culture were most strikingly illustrated by the immense number of chapels owned by individuals and intended for their private use. Other chapels were not strictly personal but belonged to small groups, such as families, fraternities or permanent fellowships. Guilds, corporations and devotional societies needed a place for their occasional prayer meetings at which a priest officiated as their spiritual director. Since few of them had enough money to build their own chapel they would ask a church to house them and space would be reserved for them near one of the altars on either side of the high altar, where the public services were held. The latter were no longer so comprehensive as they had been, for each family and household wanted to worship in a private sanctuary. Great nobles had long been accustomed to equip their castles with oratories modeled on the royal chapels. This practice was growing, for the well-to-do wanted to live like lords, with the same food, drink, clothes and recreations. Every paterfamilias who could afford it employed a chaplain to say mass at home for himself and his family. Failing that, he sought, by means of a substantial donation, to secure a reserved space in church, either in the precincts of the choir or in one of the side-aisles. He hoped in this way to show that he had bettered himself and that his descendants would sit in the seats of the mighty. The Mendicant Friars did not object to selling space in their churches to the more prominent and bountiful members of their congregation. There were no fewer than twenty-five private chapels round the choir of the Cordeliers in Paris.

These family and fraternity chapels fulfilled a double purpose. The first, or external, function consisted in holding private services and saying masses for individual members of the group. They might be living but more often were not, for this function was essentially elegiac. Worship of the dead played a major part in men's instinctual religious feeling. As the Church adopted and formalized this spontaneous emotion, so there developed the Christian rites for the departed. At this time, membership of a fraternity meant above all that a man was assured of a decent funeral and that in subsequent generations fellow-members would pray perpetually for those who were dead. The descendants of a family felt similarly beholden to those who had gone before. As yet there was no waning of belief in the efficacy of rites performed by the living on behalf of the dead. On the contrary, there was a growing conviction that death was not the end.

The Pope at Avignon had proclaimed that a man's soul appeared before God immediately after death and received a first, beatific vision of Him; but between that brief encounter and the Last Judgement, separating the damned from the elect, there stretched the wastes of Purgatory. At this stage the soul could acquire merit that it still lacked for admission to Paradise, and a man's friends could credit his account with the benefits accruing from repeated commemoration of the divine sacrifice. Every testator, therefore, assigned a considerable share of his bequests to paying for a stately funeral service and, above all, for innumerable masses to be sung in perpetuity. Such legacies, whereby families often ruined themselves, were regarded as the best insurance against hell-fire. It was also believed that the nearer masses were celebrated to the remains of the person whose salvation was at stake, the greater was their redemptive power. The most effective arrangement, therefore, was to assemble in one place the tomb, the altar and the priest who was to perform the sacrament until the end of time. The Christian who was concerned for his own and his family's salvation endowed a private chapel as soon as he could afford it. This was no light matter, for it meant buying a place of burial, fitting it up appropriately and then providing capital for the perpetual maintenance of one or two resident chaplains, constituting the chantry. There was soon an entire ecclesiastical proletariat competing for these chaplaincies, which combined a good living with very little work. The chaplain in *Canterbury Tales* is the embodiment of easy sloth. Yet the abundant supply of priests eager for these sinecures could hardly keep pace with the demand, so inordinate were the requirements of the rich as they contemplated the grave. One Gascon noble, the Captal de Buch, provided in his will for fifty thousand masses to be sung in the year of his death, plus sixty-one perpetual anniversaries and eighteen chaplaincies. These practices deprived parishes of their working clergy and, by substituting selfish modes of worship, helped to destroy the Church's communal institutions.

These funerary rites were not, however, the only function of the chapel, which, with the increase in private worship, became in addition a place for the meditation and self-communion of a more exclusive religious life. In the oratory where he was wont to pray for the souls of the departed in his family or fraternity, the believer could also encounter God and gradually, in silent adoration, raise the "spark" of his soul towards Him. His chapel would be filled with objects conducive to such outpourings and tended, like the royal chapels, to become a reliquary. The more intelligible Christianity became the more credulous was belief in the redemptive power of saintly remains. In the twelfth and thirteenth centuries the sophistication of priestly culture in churches built and organized by the higher clergy had kept the veneration of relics within reasonable bounds. In the fourteenth century the influence of laymen swept away these restraints. Relics were considered the most valuable present one could give or receive, and they, like everything else, became vulgarized. Chapels, moreover, were adorned with images designed to fortify the soul or expose it to the light of the Holy Spirit. They filled the stained-glass windows and were mingled with symbols of ownership, such as the badge or motto or portrait of the Founder. Painted or carved in wood or alabaster, they were displayed on the panels of the reredos, a group of allegorical scenes which was normally kept folded and hidden from the public, and was only opened for the private use of its owners, who also owned the chapel. These images acquired an even more clannish atmosphere in the form of statues portraying the patron saints of the family or fraternity. They were kept in cupboards and only taken out by members of the privileged coterie, either for their private contemplation or to be paraded in public as evidence of prestige.

Things of this kind were not fixtures like a tomb or an altar but, being portable, could be removed from the chapel, projecting its mystical function into everyday life. Why should exercises in loving God be reserved to special times and places? The new Christianity purported to be coterminous with the believer's entire existence. One consequence of the fourteenth-century inclination to private worship was the use of small-scale devotional objects. They provided an even more personal counterpart to the chapel and could create, anywhere and at any time, an appropriate setting for deep and devout meditation. It now became fashionable for relics to be set in jewels and carried permanently on the person of him whom they were supposed to protect from harm and fill with grace. Little diptychs or triptychs were made of precious materials. They could be opened for prayer, like a reredos, before a battle or tournament, during a business journey or in the privacy of the closet. For many laymen the psalter and breviary, likewise, became a kind of portable chapel. Their illuminations, reproducing the subjects of stained-glass window or reredos, framed the sacred text in glowing pictures, more eloquent and emotive than the Latin words of prayer. Of all these objects the most valuable were probably those which have been preserved in collections to this day. They are lavishly designed and bear an odd resemblance to fashionable toys, for which they may sometimes be mistaken. Like chapels, they could be afforded only by the wealthiest men and women; but it is apparent from inventories, wills and family papers that less costly articles of the same kind were owned by people of moderate means, such as minor officials, knights of low degree and citizens of provincial towns. At the still humbler level of the masses, an equivalent commodity was being marketed very cheaply by the end of the century, in the form of woodcuts and illustrations which could be tacked to the wall, sewn on one's clothing or folded in a pocket.

In these prints, as in ivory diptychs, illuminations and jeweled reliquaries, the devotional image always has an architectural frame, the abstract symbol of a sanctuary. The constant use of arcading, pinnacles and gables is more than a vestigial reminder of the supremacy once enjoyed by the builder's craft. It shows that to the truly religious man these objects, better suited though they were to the modern form of worship, were nonetheless a substitute, not merely for the chapel where he sometimes knelt in prayer, but also for the cathedral he had abandoned. Amid the general surrender of the Christian religion into the hands of the laity, this phantom church still stood; partly as the enduring memory of an outworn rubric, partly as the palpable symbol of an inner faith, whose sanctuary was the heart of man.

THE HOUSE OF PRAYER

The fourteenth-century Christian regarded his priest, singing Mass in the parish church, mainly as the bestower of sacraments that conferred divine blessing. Now that his faith was wholly directed towards Christ's agony, the Mass came to appear as a symbolic paraphrase of the Passion. On the instructions of Jean Chevrot, bishop of Tournai, Roger van der Weyden minutely depicted the various sacramental rites on the side-panels of a triptych. The greatest of all sacraments is the Eucharist, which brings back the Real Presence of Christ on the Cross. The central panel, therefore, is devoted exclusively to the ceremony of consecration, represented by the scene on Calvary which dominates the foreground of the whole composition. The cross stands in a huge church, airy, gleaming and supported on slender columns. Light streams through delicately tinted windows, and the building is so designed that everyone can see the slow elevation of the Host. Indeed, the priest is showing us the Body of God as he stands in the center of the chancel, beneath a reredos of the Annunciation. Behind him, concealed by the rood-screen, canons are chanting their archaic plainsong.

In England, thanks to the enduring prosperity of its landowners, the great religious houses retained their wealth until the very end of the fourteenth century. Bishops and abbots lost no time in securing their profits against grasping monarchs by investing them in huge religious edifices, which also enabled them to indulge their fondness for display. In this way sacred art flowered nobly in the traditional forms of English architecture. These buildings were not public. Converging on the choir and cloister, they were intended exclusively for monastic devotions. In the covered walks of the cloister the monks could study and meditate; here the novices were given instruction and moral lectures were delivered. It was a place of mystical communion where those dedicated to the religious life advanced towards the knowledge of God and sought to identify themselves with the suffering Christ. Each of the arches bordering the cloister marked a step on the road leading to Calvary, to the Son of God suspended from the Cross. But all the members of the monastic community assembled at regular intervals within the church for the collective prayers and chants of the canonical hours.

Between 1337 and 1357 the great roof of the choir at Gloucester Abbey was built, in the words of the chronicle, "with the alms of the faithful who flocked to the tomb" of King Edward II, widely regarded in those days as a martyr. Technical advances made it possible to knock down the end wall and build the marvelous window through which the light of the Holy Ghost poured down upon the choir of canons below.

The Mendicant Friars, too, filled their churches with light, but for a different reason. They stood open to all, for they were built, not for private prayer or the bestowing of sacraments, but for pastoral teaching and guidance. They were great, unadorned barns, plain as the poverty they exemplified and perfectly attuned to the new, communal Christianity, the brotherhood of common men. In Florence, the single nave of the Franciscan church of Santa Croce consists of an immense bare space. At the exact center of the vast nave stands the Crucifix, dominating the church, attracting all eyes, reigning over all devotional attitudes. At the east end the high altar is flanked by a number of chapels, for there were many friars in residence and each of them had to sing Mass daily. Moreover, a number of leading Florentine families succeeded in having side-chapels assigned to them for their private devotions and for the burial of their dead. These chapels, on the fringe of the monastic community, became their property, maintained and embellished by their oblations. Here austerity was felt to be out of place: the prestige of the family was at stake, and each sought to outdo the other in the quality and extent of the frescoes which it displayed on the walls and ceiling of its own chapel.

The chantry built by the Earls of Warwick is none the less isolated for being set among the pillars of the choir at Tewkesbury Abbey. It was intended that the monks, assembled in prayer before the altar, should purvey their spiritual benison to the family vault; but the sepulchre is enclosed within a stone canopy, in the likeness of a church, which effectively marks it off as a place of private devotion for the House of Warwick.

THE CHOIR OF GLOUCESTER CATHEDRAL, WEST SIDE. 1337-1357.

CHOIR OF THE CHURCH
OF SANTA CROCE, FLORENCE.

ROGER VAN DER WEYDEN (1399-1464). ALTARPIECE OF THE SEVEN SACRAMENTS, CENTRAL PANEL: CRUCIFIXION IN A CHURCH,
WITH THE OFFERING OF THE HOLY EUCHARIST IN THE BACKGROUND, ABOUT 1445. MUSÉE DES BEAUX-ARTS, ANTWERP.

CLOISTER OF WORCESTER CATHEDRAL, 3RD QUARTER OF 14TH CENTURY.

CHANTRY OF THE EARLS OF WARWICK IN TEWKESBURY ABBEY, 1422.

The entire purpose of modern worship, of *devotio moderna*, was to prepare the soul for union with the Holy Spirit, leading it gradually on and, at the critical moment of death, securing it against the perils of its journey. It therefore bade the Christian draw near to the word of God and find in it the source of constant prayer and meditation. How should a man know the Father, the Son and the Holy Ghost, except through the Scriptures? To the fourteenth-century laity direct apprehension of Holy Writ became an essential part of the religious life, as it had been since the earliest days of Christendom for monks in the seclusion of Benedictine cloisters or in the cells of the Solitary Orders. It was no longer enough for the layman to listen passively to the reading or chanting of Biblical texts; he must understand them.

The rulers of the Church, suspicious and fearful of heresy, were not anxious that laymen should read the Bible on their own, so that translations of the Old and New Testaments did not bulk large in the efforts to make Latin ecclesiastical works available to the general public. About 1340 a Yorkshire hermit put the Psalter into vernacular Anglo-Saxon. Fifty years later a number of teachers at Oxford produced two versions of the Gospels, of which one was too scholarly for the uneducated and the other was more colloquial. These translators, however, being tarred with the brush of Lollardry, were regarded as radical opponents of the higher clergy. When Jean de Cy put the Bible into French and added a commentary, he was working for the King of France, Jean le Bon. His book, sumptuously got up, was a thing of great value in itself and by no means intended for popular consumption. By the beginning of the fifteenth century there was as yet nothing in French for the educated layman beyond short extracts from the Gospels, to be read on Sundays, and a few "edifying" passages adapted from the Bible. The latter reached him mainly in the form of sermons.

The preachers did at least endeavor to speak convincingly and make their audience grasp what they meant. By mime and gesture they tried to bring the Gospels home to the masses. They acted it themselves and caused the main themes of their sermons to be depicted in *tableaux vivants* or processions. They encouraged their listeners to enact the holy tragedy either in pageants or at the meetings of fraternities, or even in the privacy of their oratories. These sacred performances made it possible to reach the humblest of the laity, whose thick heads were impervious even to the most elementary arguments of the popular preachers. And they had a deeper purpose yet. The fact that members of the congregation were expected to play an active role by singing, or rather miming, would lead them actually to live events in the life of Christ and thus to be embodied for a moment in their brother, Jesus. Medieval piety had always sought to strengthen the willingness of the soul by giving it the support of the flesh. In Benedictine monasteries prayers were never silent but were shouted in unison by the whole community. The manipulation of parchment in transcribing a sacred text also involved physical effort, in which the wrist was as active as the mind. Strenuous reading aloud took the place of inaudible mumbling. By miming the Word of God a man could best make it his own and his faith a part of his life. The Dominican, Heinrich Suso, would walk at night from one pillar of his cloister to another, enacting the passion of Christ. These stations of the Cross would lead him to the crucifix in the chapel, where he would commune with the Virgin. Exercises such as this would bring him the moments of bliss that he has recorded: "It often seemed to him that he glided through the air, adrift between time and timelessness on the unfathomable ocean of God's mystery." Were all believers to do likewise, mustered and led by the Mendicant Friars, they too would walk the mystic road towards the radiance of salvation, in which death itself was but the narrow antechamber to deliverance. At times the entire population of a town would join in a huge communal performance. In 1400, during the three days of Pentecost, the craftsmen of Avignon staged a Passion play at their own expense. "Two hundred actors were needed, with a countless host of men armed and caparisoned. Many stands for men and women were erected in the square before the monastery of the Preaching Friars. Never had there been so princely a spectacle, or one that was seen by ten or twelve thousand people." Mystery plays, which were by no means confined to the fraternities, gave rise to a ubiquitous school of drama, where every Christian was to play a part in the daily performances of his private life.

This was how the image came to predominate, for it provided the most effective stepping-stone between the word of God and the passionate miming whereby body and soul were freed from their bonds, from all that impeded their progress "towards sublime contemplation on the heights of beatitude." The image helped the novice by setting his feet on the path. "Daughter," wrote Heinrich Suso, "it is time you took wing and left the comfortable nest that images prepare for the beginner." Preachers were well aware that they must appeal to the eye of the innumerable beginners who made up their congregations. But to have a more lasting effect they must also provide features and colors that would be engraved on the memory and give the faint-hearted a source of renewed fervor long after the missionaries' departure. Bernardino of Siena had used the symbol of Jesus' name, framed in a sunburst, not merely as an illustration but as the central theme of his preaching. At his request it was engraved upon the façades of patrician mansions. The effect of penitential sermons and *sacre rappresentazioni* could be thus prolonged by painted panels, polychrome sculpture and the dissemination of holy images by means of wood-engraving. In order to bring God within reach of the masses, who were equally prone to enthusiasm and apostasy, fourteenth-century religious art became essentially histrionic.

Giotto's renown rested on the fact that he succeeded better than any of his predecessors in splendidly reproducing the various scenes of a mystery play on the walls of churches. A producer of genius, he crystallized the flow of drama and provided exemplary concepts to those who sought

to love St Francis and St Joachim, Jesus and the Virgin, and who hoped by truly knowing them to apprehend their divine nature. The Friars, those educators of the baptized who strove to impart the New Testament to the very lowest strata of Christian society, believed the image to be a far more persuasive medium than reading the Bible or hearing it read. For the benefit of the laity the fourteenth-century Bible became "graphic," consisting in a series of stories as lively and enthralling as any of the popular myths or romances. For the illiterate, likewise, it assumed the narrative form of the "Poor Man's Bible," in which the gist of the story was broken up into a number of simple, expressive pictures. Those who led this new type of ministry believed, in the words of Eustache Mercadé, the author of a *Passion* which was performed about 1430 in the North of France, that "for some who do not understand the Scriptures it is better that they should be given examples, stories and paintings on the walls of monasteries and palaces."

These were the books of ordinary folk. As religion became more popularized, it naturally became more pictorial. "Stand on Calvary and fix the eyes of thy soul diligently on all that is being inflicted on thy Lord. Watch with the eyes of thy soul how some are planting the Cross in the ground, while others are preparing the nails and hammer." In the *Meditationes vitae Christi*, attributed to St Bonaventura but certainly written at the end of the fourteenth century by a Franciscan from Tuscany, all the metaphors and the whole drift of the work show how important a part was assigned to vision in developing a man's inner life.

In those days it was universally believed that vision engendered love and nurtured it. The fabric of affection was woven by light and the eyes were the windows of the soul. In the thirteenth century Robert Grosseteste, who founded the Oxford school of philosophy, had postulated, in opposition to Aristotle, a cosmogony based on light. He believed the universe to have originated in a sudden effulgence, which begot the spheres and elements, the shapes and dimensions of matter. This doctrine, as received and amplified by Franciscan scholars, led to a reinterpretation of natural philosophy through the study of optics; but it also coincided with the Neo-Platonist strain in Western Christianity, rivaling the rational theology of Aristotle and offsetting the appeal to the intellect by its encouragement of mysticism. Was not light, God-created and life-giving, the closest link between God and His creatures? By it the divine grace was diffused and the human soul enabled to behold the face of God.

These ideas led thirteenth-century thinkers to extol the eloquent use of light in the building of cathedrals. As time went on and Christianity became the affair of ordinary men and women, the learned theories of the Oxford Franciscans were easily wedded to traditional secular beliefs. For laymen, too, believed that a man must see in order to love, and that "eyes looked love to eyes that spake again." In the songs of thirteenth-century troubadours, the spark of love is transmitted by the eye to the heart, which it sets aflame, and by this stream of light two hearts are fused in one. Flame, heart, passion, spark: the same words are found in the sermons and instructions of mystics and in the erotic songs of chivalry. Sacred and profane love came together by the same process that united priestly and knightly codes of behavior. Just as the ardor of the courtly swain was kindled by the vision of his lady, so Heinrich Suso, miming the Passion of Jesus, was drawn towards the image of Christ crucified. In a late fourteenth-century manuscript illustrating allegorically the spiritual pilgrimage of Suso, his soul may be seen, at a moment of great stress, lying prostrate before an image of Jesus on the Cross. In the sculpted groups placed over tombs or in the panel paintings of commemorative altarpieces, the donors are portrayed kneeling before the divine Man and his Mother; and in their rapt gaze the light of sacred love seems to be flooding the depths of their being.

This accounts for the great part played by the monstrance in fourteenth-century ritual and for the long pause in the mass when the Host is elevated and displayed to the people, filling them with love. For the same reason reliquaries were designed as transparent containers in which the holy remains were visible. Everyone wanted to see the objects of his mystical yearning and found in doing so relief from anguish and food for hope. Piety at this degraded level reached the point of clothing images with magic powers. Was it not enough to look at a statue of St Christopher to be sure that one would not die in sin before the day was out? People there-fore insisted on the ubiquitous presence of these barely Christian effigies. That of the good giant Christopher kept watch over every crossroads and was placed on the west wall of churches so that the faithful, glancing up at him as they went out, might carry with them the reassurance of his protection. The ecclesiastical authorities, far from discouraging the popular tendency to worship images, in some cases guaranteed their supernatural powers. Indulgences were promised to those who uttered a certain prayer before the statue of Christ during the Mass of St Gregory, or who visited the Calvary in the Charterhouse at Champmol.

Some churchmen, however, wished to condemn this form of worship and placed a ban on allegedly miraculous images. A treatise was written "against those who adore images and statues," and further attempts were made by Gerson and Cardinal Nicholas of Cusa. An English writer stated the true doctrine in measured terms: "Images are designed by the Church as calendars for the laity and the ignorant, so that they may apprehend Christ's Passion and the good life and martyrdom of saints. But if a man renders unto lifeless images the worship he owes to God, or if he places in them the faith or hope that he could place in God, then he commits the gravest sin of idolatry." The most violent and uncompromising attacks came from certain heretical groups who clung to a truly spiritual faith, cleansed of all the defilements introduced by a corrupt, affluent, worldly-minded clergy. Images were included in their outcry against the pomp of the Roman Church. In 1387 two Lollards smashed a statue of St Catherine at Leicester. Soon after, the Bohemian Puritans of Mount Tabor objected violently to ornamental figures in churches. Iconoclasm, however, never amounted to more than an explosion of heretical violence. In the main fourteenth-century art, whether monumental or in the form of small objects of private worship, consisted in the expression of an unsophisticated faith.

Representational religious art was naturally related to the written word, such as extracts from the Bible or from the lives of saints, which were often copied directly onto phylacteries or along the edge of a painting. These sequences of pictures, which could be read like the illustrated strips of modern "comics," lent vigor to the message and ensured that it received wide and lasting publicity. Their function was to make belief tangible and visible. They resorted to symbol or, more often, allegory in order to clothe the invisible in familiar dress, with all the characteristics of earthly existence. These pictures set out to portray substance as well as meaning. Since they had to display the attributes of reality, the artists of that time borrowed from antiquity a number of illusionist devices. It was also necessary that sacred figures, whose function was to uplift the soul and release it from earthly trammels, should not rub shoulders with the profane. They must be set on a higher plane, even though painters and sculptors might well depict men face to face with God in the same imaginary setting. No one would ever mistake the donor for the Christ he is adoring, or even for the patron saint who stands protectively behind him. They belong to different worlds, separated by a barrier that can only be crossed at the fearful moment of death. To symbolize this paramount segregation, Giotto used certain theatrical effects, such as the abstract blue of his background in scenes that are outside the normal scheme of time. He also made great use of the stately manner which the rediscovery of Roman art had taught him. It is true that the characters in his solemn drama have the appearance of men. Joachim sleeps like any shepherd. Yet something undefinable would prevent one slapping him on the back—some invisible barrier like that which separates the actor from his audience, or the communicant from the priest carrying the Eucharist, or Don Giovanni from the statue of the Commendatore. Even in the most trumpery altarpiece, painted for some craftsmen's guild in a humble parish, figures from the Bible are never demeaned to the level of prosaic existence. In the religious art of this period there is always a point where unshaken belief in another world brings realism to a halt.

The hereafter, real but unseen, is disclosed, even before the dreaded revelation of death, by images presaging the radiance of divine love. For it is inhabited by a multitude of minor characters, the company of Saints. They, like the demons and evil spirits whom they harried, figured prominently in the religion of ordinary people. Despite their numbers, these mediators could be clearly distinguished from one another, and the more skillful artists, when portraying them in groups, tried to identify them individually. Each had his favorite habitat in this world, his abode in life and the resting-place of his mortal remains, and it was here that his miracles were performed. Each had his own powers, to be invoked in special circumstances, and his story was recorded in the great romance compiled for Christendom, Jacobus de Voragine's *Golden Legend*. The saints were recognized by their features, dress and symbolic accessories, so that Joan of Arc had not the slightest doubt which ones were announcing her vocation. The imagery, like the processions, of Christianity attached great importance to powers that warded off the more alarming forms of death, whether the recognized protector of a guild or class, such as the valiant horseman and lancer St George, the patron saint of knights, or the personal guardian to whom every Christian entrusted his body and soul. Images enabled the newly canonized, like St Thomas Aquinas or St Catherine of Siena, to attain celebrity, and the Church used its control over images to restrain the cruder forms of worship which grew up around these subordinate characters. The paintings at Assisi were so arranged as to place St Francis firmly within the official bosom of the Church.

The center of the devotional stage, however, was always occupied by the commanding figure of God: God in three persons, for many fourteenth-century fraternities took the Trinity as their patron, so that painters and sculptors were told to portray the three divine powers. Militant Christians, at their most enterprising, laid special emphasis on the Holy Ghost. Many of them believed, like the Little Brothers of St Francis, that His kingdom had come, and in the eyes of all Christians He determined the relationship between a man's soul and the Godhead. Yet in pictures of the Trinity the dove of the Holy Ghost always appears as an accessory, a sort of poetic hyphen. Even God the Father is relegated to the background as a symbol of majesty. The whole scene is dominated by the crucified Son. Prolonged Franciscan influence had resulted in fourteenth-century portraiture gravitating towards the source of love, the image of God made Man in the person of Jesus, brother and saviour. But which Jesus was this? In Romanesque tympana the Benedictines had portrayed Christ of the Advent coming at the Last Trump in the blinding radiance of His glory to judge the quick and the dead. Over the west door of cathedrals thirteenth-century philosophers had set Jesus the Doctor, book in hand as he expounded from his Chair. But the Christ adored by common men was Himself a man. He was a man who touched the heart, for the modern form of worship consisted in "a compassion that is close to tears." This was the Jesus whom the preachers described and the *sacre rappresentazioni* mimed, the Jesus of Christmas and Easter. He was a God of fable, a character in a story, this Christ who shared with poor men the helplessness of being a baby and the desolation of dying.

Christmas and Easter. The winter feast is one of joy, a cockcrow of hope at the blackest hour of the night. That joy, with its sweet message of comfort, pertains even more to the Mother than to the Child in the manger. As Christianity became more popular and more accessible to women, it developed rather sentimental variations on the Marian theme, which had in any case been thoroughly explored by the Church. First came Mary startled at her prayers by the angel of the Annunciation; then Mary kneeling before her new-born Son; then Mary watching Him at play among the smooth lawns and bright flowers of the Mystic Garden. Lastly there was the Virgin panoplied and raised in majesty above the company of Saints, assuming their protective role and, as sole Mediatrix, gathering all Christians beneath her blue mantle. Then, after the sackcloth and ashes of Lent, Easter was ushered in "with travail and holy sorrow." Only by untold suffering could Christ lead men to salvation. No spectacle in that age exerted a stronger appeal than the Passion; no symbol was more venerated than the Cross, the tragic kernel of a poor man's faith. Gradually the vision shifted, from Christ mocked and flogged to Christ nailed on the Cross, Christ dead. The Virgin was no longer the serene mother of the flowery meadows, of the Coronation or the Assumption; she was now the Virgin of pity, contributing to the act of redemption by the intensity of grief and the agony of love as she held in her lap the broken, lifeless body of her Son. The first representation of the Holy Sepulchre was carved in 1419 for the enactment of His burial on the stage. To mime the life of Jesus and behold its various episodes; "to watch with the eyes of one's soul how some were planting the Cross in the ground, while others were preparing the nails and hammer"; to become so rapt in this vision as actually to receive the Stigmata: all this was part of men's yearning to draw so near to Him that at last they might vanquish death as He had done. The imitation of Christ was wholly inspired by fear of eternal darkness and the hope of resurrection.

RELICS, IMAGES AND OTHER DEVOTIONAL OBJECTS

Since royal chapels were intended primarily to house the relics of saints, themselves encased in the most costly materials, they became repositories for jewelry and all manner of liturgical accessories. Every sovereign felt that he ought to bring his people nearer to salvation by adding to his collection. In the France of Charles VI, however, this aspect of royal piety was already tending towards mannerism, extravaganza and courtly display. Reliquaries became so ornate and were so artfully designed as to have a festive or theatrical air. One, for instance, is a glittering pyramid of gold, enamel and gems, displaying a host of tiny figures: God the Father, the Virgin in majesty, Jesus the Saviour and all their attendant apostles and tutelary saints. The increasing popularity of capitular art led to greater insistence on realism. The ordinary Christian wanted everything to be made plain. He expected the story of God and the saints to be told and illustrated so vividly that his own devotional response would be almost automatic. When the Florentine guilds decorated the new oratory of Orsanmichele, or when the people of Orvieto provided a splendid receptacle for their most precious relic, the Corporal, a piece of cloth stained with the blood of Christ, lifelike images combined with unstinted riches to enshrine the hallowed object.

Meanwhile the preaching friars were urging men to make spiritual exercises part of their everyday life. The tendency for prayer to become both personal and continuous led to a demand for smaller, more private objects. The Parisian workers in ivory produced miniature statues and altarpieces, in which the holy tragedy was enacted by a few figures in a diptych. To the devout this was as eloquent as the pulpit at Pisa, and it would go easily in a traveling-chest. By the end of the fourteenth century the triptych had become a locket. It provided the worthy Christian with a handsome ornament and enabled him to wear a relic on his person. When opened, it revealed an image of God in His suffering. This portable shrine, stamped with the symbol of the Passion, marks the end of a long process whereby, in the course of a century, the treasured objects of faith, once displayed to all in the Church's ceremonies, had gradually fallen into the strong grasp of the mighty who coveted jewels.

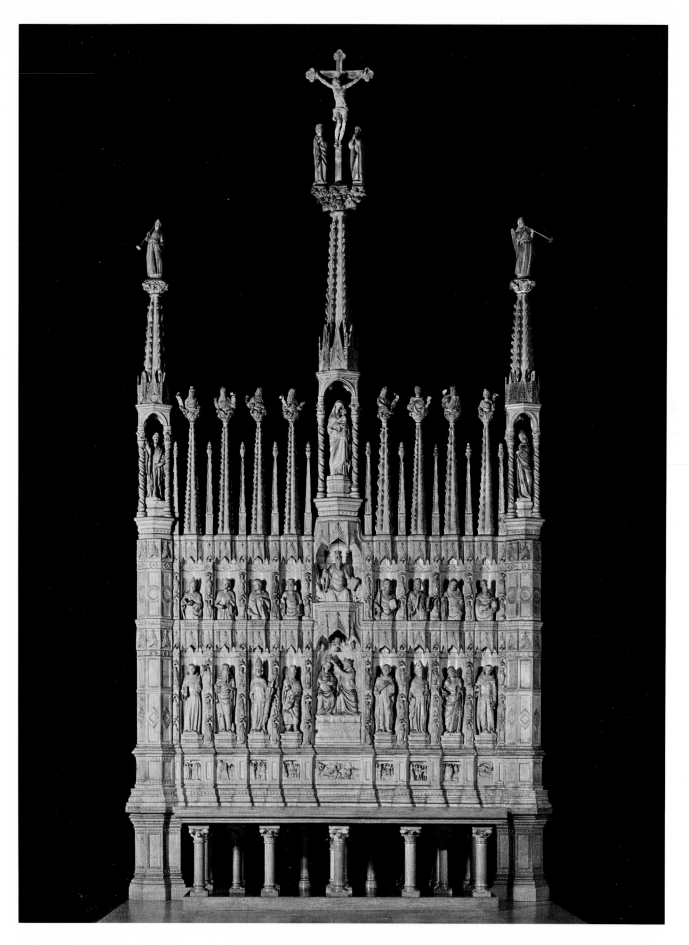

JACOBELLO (DIED ABOUT 1409) AND PIER PAOLO (DIED 1403?) DALLE MASEGNE. MARBLE ALTAR, 1388-1392.
CHURCH OF SAN FRANCESCO, BOLOGNA.

UGOLINO DI VIERI (ACTIVE 1329-1385). SILVER-GILT SHRINE OF THE CORPORAL, 1337.
CAPPELLA DEL CORPORALE, ORVIETO CATHEDRAL.

NICOLA PISANO (ABOUT 1220-BEFORE 1284).
PULPIT, 1260. BAPTISTERY, PISA.

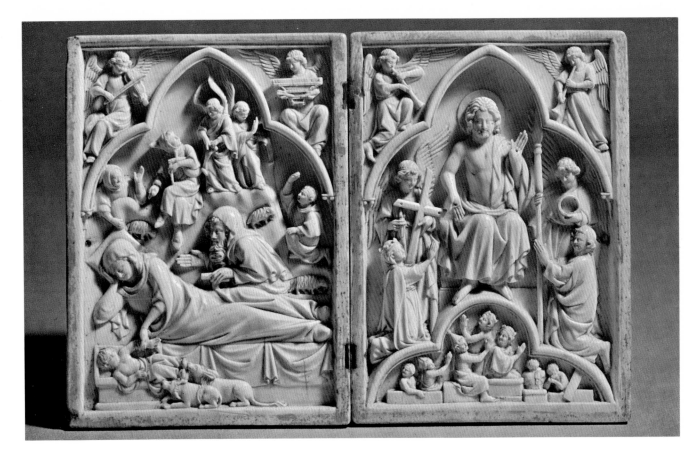

THE NATIVITY AND THE LAST JUDGEMENT. IVORY DIPTYCH OF THE FIRST HALF OF THE 14TH CENTURY.
FRENCH WORKMANSHIP. LOUVRE, PARIS.

LOCKET IN THE FORM OF A TRIPTYCH REPRESENTING CHRIST CROWNED WITH THORNS.
ABOUT 1400. SCHATZKAMMER DER RESIDENZ, MUNICH.

RELIQUARY OF THE CHAPEL OF THE HOLY GHOST. FRANCE, EARLY 15TH CENTURY. LOUVRE, PARIS.

THE DEATH OF GOD

Fourteenth-century piety reached an emotional climax when the suffering and death of Christ were portrayed in countless images of Calvary. In the imitation of Jesus Christ men were led to share His sorrows, witness His agony and thus to pass with Him through death and be raised by Him to glory. This was the one hope that enabled Christians in those days to look death in the face. Once Christianity became part of ordinary men's lives, both the Franciscans' call to repentance and the horror of the laity at seeing the flower of knightly zest fade and shrivel, combined to bring them to the foot of the Cross. Harshly it dominated the whole of religious symbolism.

The mode of portraying this tragic theme was formulated in the teaching of Assisi, where Pietro Lorenzetti was among the first to give it full expression. His painting shows the bare Cross, the torrents of blood, the wounded hands and side, the pincers that ripped the nail from His torn feet, and His poor, stark body, pathetically distorted. It was Lorenzetti who first depicted Mary and the disciples bending over the broken corpse and fervently kissing it.

When Philip Duke of Burgundy planned his own resting-place in the Charterhouse of Champmol, he commissioned a great crucifix in which painting and sculpture should combine to give the dead Christ every semblance of reality. Together, Claus Sluter and Jean Malouel strove to attain a degree of pathos to which the admirable head of Christ, no longer colored, still bears testimony. In this case the Cross was placed above a spring, the healing Fount of Life; and the prince's tomb, setting death at naught, blithely extolled the Trinity and almighty God.

In order to counteract the teaching of those heretical Franciscans who proclaimed that the kingdom of the Holy Ghost was approaching, the Church laid special emphasis on the mystery of one God in three persons. Thus the Holy Spirit was widely depicted in conjunction with the Crucifixion. God was seated in majesty on the "throne of salvation"; the dove of the Holy Spirit wore the countenance of the Son and upheld His Cross. In 1427 Masaccio painted this subject at Santa Maria Novella, placing it in the semblance of a chapel, with a masterly likeness of a skeleton beneath. The sublimity of the composition consists in the figure of Jesus on the Cross. The two donors are set apart, kneeling on either side of the picture, and their expressions deliberately exclude them from the world where the divine figures of the Virgin and

St John dwell in motionless eternity. Yet they are all drawn to the same scale and have the same monumental rigidity. In this way the donors are raised above the common level of mankind and are beatified by divine grace.

Meanwhile, Christ rose triumphant from the tomb. The power of the Resurrection required for its portrayal a dynamism which, it would seem, the patrons of that time seldom encouraged in their artists. Formerly religious art had strained after spiritual perfection, but the more humdrum piety of the fourteenth century was doubtless too down-to-earth to leap the grim abyss of death. The painters of chapels could do justice to the love and anguish of men, and their imaginative power enabled them even to imbue with grandeur their visions of the Last Judgement; but they were no good at portraying supernal bliss, and their scenes of Paradise were usually absurd.

There was one painter, however, who succeeded in endowing the Risen Christ with an invincible force, representing him as the dauntless hero of a victory over the powers of darkness and the fears that beset mankind: this was the unknown master of the Bohemian altarpiece from Trebon. This Christ might almost be the figurehead of that burning faith which was soon to inspire the Hussites. Nothing could contrast more strongly with the figure of the resurrected Lazarus in the Très Riches Heures. *The latter is truly a man, splendid of countenance and physique, with the clean-cut solidity of a classical bronze. Here the Limbourgs were holding out to the ageing Jean de Berry the traditional promise of knightly optimism, combined with the first-fruits of Italian humanism. In both cases it was an earthly promise.*

This concept could only have flourished in the hot-house, sophisticated atmosphere of 1400, when court life at Paris achieved an amazing brilliance, compounded of pomp, sensibility, eagerness and elegance, soon to be blighted by war. The ordinary man's attitude to death, not only that preached by the friars to their awestruck followers, but also the attitude of the stern, ascetic Christians for whom Masaccio worked, was one of terror or solemnity. A man's funeral did not portend his return to familiar pleasures; it was a farewell, a final rite for a corpse doomed to corruption. Only for the Virgin could it be a happy farewell, as angels decked her body with garlands for the coming Assumption. It was Mary rather than her Son whose death comforted the devout.

CLAUS SLUTER (DIED 1406). CRUCIFIX FROM THE CHARTREUSE DE CHAMPMOL (DETAIL), 1395-1399. MUSÉE ARCHÉOLOGIQUE, DIJON.

PIETRO LORENZETTI (ABOUT 1280-1348). THE DESCENT FROM THE CROSS, ABOUT 1329-1331.
FRESCO, LOWER CHURCH OF SAN FRANCESCO, ASSISI.

MASACCIO (1401-1429). THE TRINITY, WITH THE VIRGIN, JOHN THE BAPTIST AND DONORS, 1427.
BELOW, A SKELETON ON A SARCOPHAGUS. FRESCO, SANTA MARIA NOVELLA, FLORENCE.

LIFE AFTER DEATH

Fourteenth-century Christianity was more a matter of making a good end than of living a good life, and the chapel was the scene not so much of prayer and contemplation as of a funerary cult. Religious feeling, owing to its increasingly popular and secular nature, was overshadowed by the idea of death. As a result of showing the ordinary man's emotions and his dread of the unknown that lay beyond the grave, Christianity was bound to ask plain, disconcerting questions. What has happened to the dead? Where are they? Do not mysterious lights and unwonted sounds reflect their presence, separate and invisible yet close at hand and full of menace? Do they not crowd uneasily at the threshold of consciousness? Are they not in league with the powers of darkness and must they not, likewise, be propitiated by deference and dutiful oblations?

The teaching of the Church at its most exalted gave an answer that would dispel these fears. Death was but the strait through which man passed from his voyage on earth to reach his last haven. The day would come, and might come soon, when "time must have a stop." Christ would return in glory and man's body would be raised incorruptible. Then the good would be separated from the wicked and the resurrected host would make their way in two groups, one to eternal bliss, the other to eternal damnation. Meanwhile the dead would sleep peacefully in an abode of Elysian calm. This was what the burial service taught, and the medieval Church, at the zenith of its power, had persecuted and stamped out the pagan rites of sepulture. It had threatened with condign punishment those who persisted in taking food to the dead, and it had stripped tombs of jewels, clothing, weapons and all the elaborate furniture placed beside the dead man, to ensure that he enjoyed his ghostly existence and did not pester the living with his wants. Men went to their last sleep naked and destitute. An extraordinary restraint was observed. Not a single ornament or emblem was placed beside the Caro-lingian princesses interred beneath the foundations of the basilica of St Gertrude at Nivelles; and when archaeologists opened the only inviolate tomb of a French king, that of Philip I at Saint-Benoît-sur-Loire, they found nothing by the body but a simple covering of leaf-work.

The clergy, however, had to come to terms with popular beliefs that were too strong to be ignored. At Cluny, as early as the tenth century, they had begun to show greater latitude in the office for the dead, by permitting the living to bring them gifts in the form of prayers and expiatory rites. Gradually, moreover, they accepted the myth of an interval between death and the Day of Judgement, during which the souls of the departed, roused from their sleep, might lead a more active life. Those whom Dante visited were by no means wrapped in slumber. Under the hesitant supervision of the Church the domain of Purgatory was recaptured by pre-Christian attitudes to death. This was precisely the area that was extended in the latter part of the thirteenth century, when the priestly grip on religious observance was loosened and the devoted labors of the Mendicant Friars brought Christianity to the common man.

The Church's traditional reluctance to allow any but princes, prelates and saints to be buried within the sanctuary was gradually overcome by the people's determination that their dead should lie as near as possible to the altar. The obsequies of the wealthy were accompanied by every luxury that money could buy, for they must enter the kingdom of the dead with all the trappings of their rank. Since a man's power was reckoned by the number of his "friends"—those who were beholden to him and owed him allegiance—his bier was attended by his entire household, followed by the poor who had been his almsmen. Finally, his tomb was adorned with images, so that he might at least avoid total oblivion by surviving in effigy.

The determination, contrary to the Christian spirit of abnegation, to go on living within the tomb evinced a worldly, possibly more fundamental instinct; the desire to overcome the dissolution of the body and man's fear, not merely of the dead, but of his own death, of Death itself. From the beginning the Church sought to harness this instinct to its own ends and had always urged men to meditate upon the putrefaction of their bodies; for this revealed the hollowness and imperfection of the flesh, condemning the ephemeral pleasures here below and challenging men to renounce the world and follow the true path of God. The skeleton and the decomposing corpse were among the most eloquent symbols of preachers calling to repentance. A constant theme of the *laudi* sung by Italian fraternities was the desolation of the dead body, consigned to the worms, and darkness of the grave. This lesson was reinforced by imagery based on the poem of the Three Dead and the Three Living. It depicts three horsemen who come upon three open graves, and in the stench of their rotting corpses the living men are suddenly confronted by the vanity of this world. The putrefying flesh, crawling with worms, bore witness, firstly, to the close connection between sin and the flesh. It was believed that only the bodies of saints were incorruptible, and when the Preaching Friars opened the tomb of St Dominic they sniffed anxiously for the fragrant "odor of sanctity" that would prove the founder of their Order to have been truly one of the blessed. Secondly, the sight of decomposing flesh admonished the Christian to live prudently and maintain himself always, like the Wise Virgins, in a state of grace; for Death was an archer who fired without warning and struck his victim in an unguarded moment. Among the symbols of Christian ritual the vision of a decaying corpse constituted a sort of barricade against the insidious charms of a beguiling but accursed world.

The increasingly secular outlook of the early fourteenth century led to a complete reversal of this argument. The great fresco in the Campo Santo at Pisa places the picture of the Three Living and the Three Dead immediately next to that of the Triumph of Death, whose purport is the exact opposite. Death brandishing his scythe, swoops furiously down upon the pleasance where, amid all the refinements of courtesy, a group of fashionable ladies and gentlemen are extolling the delights of love and the good things of this world. He will cut short their revels and, like the plague or the Black Death, fling this gay company onto his growing heap of corpses. In this case the picture no longer symbolizes the vanity of mortal pleasures; it is man's scream of terror at the remorseless doom that awaits him. The startled horses, rearing away from the dead men in their open graves, are expressive of withdrawal and abnegation; whereas the heedless lovers, unaware of the whirling fury about to annihilate their bliss, are hungry for the sweets of life. For them, as for the troubadours to whose songs they dance, the world is a fine and pleasant place; it is unthinkable that they shall have to leave it. Death, Petrarch's *donna involta in vesta negra*, is portrayed at Pisa about 1350 as riding the wings of the storm; at Palermo a century later, as bestriding the skeleton of a mare. These portents of a dreaded, ineluctable triumph themselves reflect the triumphant lusting after fleshly happiness as fourteenth-century society discarded priestly ethics. When man rose from his knees he found himself facing Death no bigger than himself, the grim figure of his own death.

The new symbols appeared nonetheless on the walls of churches, for the preachers, in calling men to a devout life, were unable to quench their love of this world or to stem the strong current of optimism among the laity. They therefore attempted in their teaching to exploit the emotional flaw in this optimism, namely the horror of Death, who blots out all human joy. The frescoes at Pisa illustrate, as it were, a sermon purporting to strengthen an argument that had lost its force by means of another, infinitely more disconcerting because it explored the tragic depths of a keener sensibility. In this way a new form of the macabre came to dominate religious art by the end of the fourteenth century. About 1400 there appeared in Germany the first collections of prints entitled *Ars moriendi*. They depicted the various stages of a man's death-agony, when he is racked with regret for the world he must leave and beset by devils who make one last assault on him but are finally routed by Christ the Brother, the Virgin and the saints. It was about this time, probably in France, that the *Danse macabre* began to take shape. Popular superstition sometimes envisaged the triumph of Death as a magic flute-player whose artful piping swept away in an irresistible dance all sorts and conditions of men, young and old, rich and poor, popes, emperors, knights and princes. Preachers may have taught their listeners to enact this grisly tarantella of triumph, which was later incorporated into devotional imagery. In 1424 the new symbol of mortality was erected at Paris in the cemetery of the Innocents, not far from the group portraying the Three Living and the Three Dead, which had been placed there by the Duc Jean de Berry but had by now lost much of its effectiveness. The *Danse macabre*, expressing so vividly the anguish of man's destiny, soon made its impact everywhere, from Coventry to Lübeck, from Nuremberg to Ferrara. It gave a final turn of the screw to his foreboding, which no longer contemplated a remote and shadowy Day of Judgement but the present reality of "Death's pale flag." "Whoso dies, dieth unto grief." Death was not the drowsy calm of the seafarer coming safe to port; it was the yawning of a bottomless pit. The ascendancy of the macabre owed nothing to scourges of the age—war, pestilence or want; it was rather the outcome of two centuries during which Christian dogma had gradually come into line with the piety of simple men. Their fear of death did not mean that they had fallen from grace or faltered in belief, but rather that Christianity had grown less eclectic and now embraced humble folk who were steadfast in their faith but could not carry it into the realm of abstract vision. The *Danse macabre*, like the Italian concept of the Triumph of Death or the image of Christ lying dead in His Mother's lap, had little in common with the piety of monks or university professors; it expressed the religion of poor men who said their prayers among the tombs of chapels or Franciscan churches.

Once the idea of death at its crudest became the central and dominant feature of religion, it was natural that, through fear of dying and the yearning for resurrection, the imitation of Jesus Christ should concentrate mainly on His death. Hence, the tomb acquired great significance, and fourteenth-century patrons were mainly concerned with funerary display. This was the object of the most numerous and detailed commissions awarded to artists. All wills began by stipulating where the testator's remains were to lie buried until Judgement Day. People who intended to build a chapel, decorate it and provide capital for its maintenance regarded it as a place of burial rather than of prayer. It was customary to plan, build and adorn one's tomb long beforehand, and even to detail the arrangements for one's own funeral. The latter was regarded as the last and undoubtedly the greatest festival of a man's life. A festival was an occasion for lavish display, and the obsequies of those days were staged with a profusion of pomp in which money was no object.

"This is how the King (the unhappy Charles VI of France, in 1422, the lowest ebb of the Hundred Years War) was carried to Notre-Dame. Four of the bishops and abbots wore the white mitre, among them the new Bishop of Paris, who waited in the doorway of Saint-Paul to sprinkle the King's body with holy water before the procession started. All except him entered the church—the Mendicant Orders, the whole University and all the colleges, the Parlement, the Châtelet and the common people. Then he was taken from Saint-Paul and the attendants began to mourn loudly. He was borne to Notre-Dame *as the body of Our Lord is borne* on the feast of St Saviour. Six of those closest to the King carried a gold canopy above his body, which itself was borne on the shoulders of thirty of his servants. They may well have been more, for he was no light weight. He lay on a bed, wearing a gold crown and grasping in one hand the royal sceptre, and in the other the Hand of Justice. Its two gold fingers raised in blessing were so long that they almost touched his crown. Before him walked the Mendicant Orders and the University, the churches of Paris, then Notre-Dame and finally the Palace. They were singing, but no one else. All the people standing in the streets or at windows were weeping and crying out as if each one saw before him the dead body of his most dearly beloved. Seven bishops were present, and the abbots of Saint-Denis and Saint-Germain-des-Prés, of Saint-Magloire, Saint-Crépin and Saint-Crépinien. All the priests and clergy were in one body, and lords of the Palace, the Provost, the Chancellor and the rest, in another. Before them walked the poor serving-men dressed in black, weeping and wailing and carrying two hundred and fifty torches; and still further in front were eighteen criers of the dead. There were twenty-four holy crosses, preceded by men ringing handbells. Behind the body walked the Duke of Bedford, alone, unaccompanied by any of the royal princes of France. In this manner the dead King was taken on Monday to Notre-Dame, where two hundred and fifty torches were burning. The Office for the Dead was sung, followed early next morning by Mass. Thereafter the same procession was formed and he was buried beside his father and mother. More than eighteen thousand persons were there, of low and high degree. Each man received sixteen silver pence, and food was provided for all." This was, of course, the funeral of a very great prince, but in those days everyone longed to be able to command such a display for himself. The interest of this narrative is that it describes not only the ceremony but also the images with which royal tombs were now beginning to be adorned.

The main object of fourteenth-century funerary art was to perpetuate the religious drama that had been enacted round the dead man's body. His tomb, set against the wall or placed in the center of the chapel, was no longer a plain sarcophagus; it had become a replica of the state bed on which his corpse had been exhibited during the funeral. It bore a life-size effigy of the dead man, protected by a processional canopy like that carried above the Host at Corpus Christi. With a view to its prolonged exposure during the obsequies, the corpse had been embalmed and its viscera removed, frequently to be dispersed and interred in various sanctuaries. Sometimes the body itself was replaced by a facsimile in leather, or even by a living impersonator. The recumbent figure on the tomb had the air of a mummy, with its display of painted features and all the emblems of power. Beneath the arcature of a symbolic church, the funeral procession was reproduced on the sides of the tomb or on its enclosure: the officiating clergy, the family in mourning and crowd of poor men carrying lights as a token of fervent prayer, before receiving a last gift of alms in food and money. The dead man was indeed a prince who must show himself once more in majesty to his people and had therefore bidden them for the last time to a feast. His burial was also an act of propitiation, which the figures on his tomb were supposed to perpetuate. Finally, the prince became one with Christ, who at His second coming would lead him to eternal life. The iconography of his tomb, therefore, was completed by a symbol of redemption, sometimes the Easter Sepulchre but more often the Resurrection.

Very few Christians could appoint such monuments of luxury and ambition for their resting-place. Most of them ended in the anonymity of the charnel-house. Those with a little money ordered from funerary masons, who did a thriving trade, plain slabs on which the effigy was simply engraved and the liturgical text was reduced to a few phrases. But the prince's tomb, like his funeral, was what everyone would really have liked. It expressed and gave reality to the popular ideal of sepulchral pomp. In layout and design it gave a clearer image of death, whose novel features were gradually incorporated into funerary art.

When the former simplicity of tombs gave way to embellishments of this kind (a process which began in thirteenth-century England and Spain) for a long time the grand tradition of religious art was maintained. The clergy allowed recumbent figures but insisted that they should be hieratic and untroubled. The features of the French kings whom Louis IX caused to be sculpted at Saint-Denis are radiant with the serenity imparted by the last rites of the Church. Delivered from "the weariness, the fever and the fret," transfigured by the supernal beauty of a body prepared for Resurrection, they lie, open-eyed, in the sweet tranquillity of timeless sleep. They have passed through the waters of death and have reached the shores of eternity and peace. To the chanting of priests they have entered the rationally ordained realm of the supernatural as it was then conceived by Aristotelian metaphysics. The close of the thirteenth century witnessed the disruption of this composure by the influx of secular emotion. It destroyed the serenity of the dead, their impassive disdain for this world, and brought them back to the anguished reality of the living. It is true that in the Gothic North effigies on tombs long retained their marmoreal calm. Although that of Philip III of France, sculpted between 1298 and 1307, is to some extent a true portrait, the dead king is imbued with an aura of solemn majesty that is not of this world. In Italy, however, where recumbent figures had previously been unknown, a new approach can be seen in the first deliberately personified sculpture on a tomb. When, soon after 1282, Arnolfo di Cambio portrayed Cardinal Guillaume de Braye in the Dominican church at Orvieto, he visualized a more human, more earthly type of majesty, which became a model for later Italian sculptors. The art of Etruria and Rome, which they gradually revived, had itself been concerned mainly with the dead. But in this case the dead were not sleeping in a state of grace while awaiting resurrection; they wanted to live on in this world, surrounded by their temporal majesty. In Tuscany and Latium, at Naples, Verona and Milan, and later still in countries beyond the Alps, the tombs of secular and pontifical princes developed into elaborate mausoleums. The revival of the Roman cult, coupled with the ordinary Christian's horror of death, led to a number of variations on the central, liturgical effigy, stretched out on its catafalque: figures paralyzed with fear, for instance, or kneeling in prayer, or bravely mounted on a charger. That the dead should be portrayed in such attitudes as these shows how funerary art was being increasingly dominated by a purely secular mentality.

*

The hairy, rotting corpse of Cardinal de Lagrange or the meticulously anatomized skeleton painted by Masaccio in Santa Maria Novella revealed precisely what lay beneath the bedizened mummy on the tombstone. The image of *Memento mori* was still in the true tradition of religious thought. Like the Three Dead Men, it showed the hollowness of a world doomed to dust and corruption. Patrons who ordered such works undoubtedly wished, on the brink of the grave, to show their contempt for the flesh, their desire to rid themselves of it and make of their tomb an act of piety and humility, a call to repentance. The portrayal of corruption on tombstones merely echoed the Church's ancient bidding to renounce the vanities of this world; but it might also awaken in the beholder an obsession with the triumph of death. In this sense the image of abject fear was bound up with the grinning, nightmare procession of the *Danse macabre*.

Donors would sometimes ask the artist to portray them, no longer peacefully sleeping with the nameless multitude of the blessed, but in a more lifelike pose and with their own features delineated. Often they would not be recumbent on a bier but in the more active posture of prayer, or even, like the Emperor Henry VII on his tomb at Pisa, seated and holding court, surrounded by statues of his counsellors, who themselves were still alive. In this they were actuated by more worldly motives. They wanted, firstly, to focus attention on themselves. People must realize that it was not just anyone's grave, but theirs; for the building of a fine tomb in one's own lifetime was proof of social success, and the whole object of an artistic showpiece was to identify the man responsible for it. Besides, the tomb

was now addressed to the living. Its occupant demanded that the passer-by should pray for him and his salvation, and this selfish tendency in piety was also reflected by the desire to affix a personal seal to one's tomb. In most cases, where flatstones were bought ready-made from craftsmen who turned them out by the dozen, a name or heraldic symbol sufficed to identify the deceased. Important patrons, however, wanted to have recognizable effigies of themselves. When the tomb had not been prepared in its owner's lifetime, the sculptor's task was sometimes simplified by the death-mask used in the funeral procession. In this way the features of recumbent figures gave fourteenth-century artists a coveted opportunity to study adventitious details.

The desire to personalize one's sepulchral monument was accompanied by another purpose, less deliberate perhaps, but equally incompatible with the spirit of abnegation. If a man's countenance were carved in stone it would be immune to the ravages of death and he would win a lasting victory over the forces of dissolution. The same victory was proclaimed by the idealized features of thirteenth-century effigies; but in their case it belonged to the life hereafter, and men also wanted to survive in their mortal guise. Sometimes the living person of the deceased was recalled at his funeral by a kind of charade. When Bertrand Du Guesclin was buried at Saint-Denis "he was depicted as he had been in life by four men armed from head to foot and mounted on well-caparisoned chargers." The funerary portraits of fourteenth-century Christians came to assume something of the magic function ascribed to those of ancient Rome. The dead man would kneel in effigy on the massive tiers of his sepulchre; or he would be throned in majesty, like Ferdinand of Castile, in Seville, at the end of the thirteenth century; or later still, like King Robert of Naples at Santa Chiara, he would appear in his normal garb and likeness. In every case the image implied victory over the mortal fear it abjured.

These portraits became more and more common. Before long they were found not only on tombs but also on altarpieces where they stood beside God and the saints, only in a more lifelike and fleshly guise. Gradually they encroached on spaces hitherto reserved by liturgical art for sacred figures. The Emperor Charles IV decided to have his own portrait on the walls of the lower chapel at Karlstein

The Comte d'Evreux can be recognized in one of the finest windows of the Cathedral, a place where formerly the prophets had stood in unapproachable majesty. Statues of ordinary men were erected against the very walls of churches. To gratify his sovereign, Cardinal de Lagrange ordered for Amiens Cathedral images of King Charles V and his counsellor Bureau de la Rivière, of the Dauphin and the King's younger son, and of himself. On the façade of Bordeaux Cathedral the statues of Christ and the apostles were replaced by those of the Pope and his cardinals. Three hundred years earlier Cluniac monks, timidly and in fear of committing sacrilege, had ventured to place the awful countenance of the Lord at the entrance to sanctuaries. Now, on the threshold of such holy places as the Convent of the Celestines, the Collège de Navarre or the Charterhouse of Champmol, there appeared the benevolent features of princes and princesses—Charles V of France, Philip the Bold of Burgundy, and their wives. In churches the angels had to make way for the faces of mortals, especially of important men who were determined that a part of themselves should survive. The age of portraiture began with these new men and their discovery of the grimness of death.

There is not much likeness to the "tyrant" Can Grande della Scala in the heroically stylized knight who rides on the apex of his mausoleum at Verona; but the figure is an even more resounding manifesto of man's ascendancy and prestige. It was inspired by two ambitions that engendered the hope of earthly survival. The first was certainly of Roman origin. Already it had been the practice for pro-

fessors who taught Roman law at Bologna, and were the first in the Middle Ages to kindle the flame of classical learning, openly to build themselves a sarcophagus, in the form of a stele, on unconsecrated ground. They sought to perpetuate their memory by having themselves portrayed in full panoply at their lecterns, presiding over their classes. The tone of an imperial triumph was echoed by the equestrian statue of Can Grande, copied by other members of the Scaliger dynasty and, after Milan's conquest of Verona, by Bernabò Visconti. The art of political magnificence, borrowed from the Caesars by Frederick II when he built Capua, culminated, among these municipal principalities and the public memorials to their lords, in the first monuments of the secular State. These princes secured temporal immortality in death. But on the marches of Roman Italy a torrent of knightly legend poured down from the Alpine passes. The valley of the Adige led by way of the Brenner to Bamberg, the seat of another Empire, Christian and Teutonic, chivalrous but feudal, still inspired by the heroes of the French "gestes," Roland, Oliver and Perceval. Can Grande and Bernabò wanted to be, not merely triumphant Caesars, but valiant knights. The victory commemorated in their statues was won in the tiltyard. Their knightly fame lives on in the echo, to be heard even in the boudoir, of their prowess and panoply of arms. They also wanted to be St George, spitting the dragon of death on their shining lances. In this new sepulchral art the recumbent figure of prayer and the dread warning of terror were challenged by the knight, flushed with his victory.

3

THE TOMB

For a long time it was the rule to allow none but
saints to be interred within the church itself: the
place of rest which the office for the dead besought
God to grant to the mouldering flesh till the Day of
Resurrection, had to be in the churchyard outside.
But once the clergy had compounded with the
common belief in an after-life, once it had admitted
that after the death of the body the soul could still
receive grace and reap spiritual advantage from
periodic funeral services, it was clear to all that
those souls fared best whose bodies lay closest to
the altar, near the sacred relics, where they could
get the full benefit of the church services. Prelates
and grandees accordingly arranged to be interred
inside the church. At first their tombs were incon-
spicuous. Then their sarcophagi and tombstones
were embellished with inscriptions and ornaments;
soon it was quite common for them to bear an
effigy of the dead man, whose memory it was the
artist's task to perpetuate. In the fourteenth century
the creation of such works passed out of the Church's
control altogether into the hands of laymen; more
and more chapels were endowed and decorated
by princes and lords, who vied with each other in
ostentation; more and more concessions were made
to popular superstition in which the preoccupation
with death bulked large. As a result religious art
tended to focus itself on the funeral monument.

The burial service sped the deceased on his way towards salvation. It had its natural counterpart in the Easter service—the rites that celebrate the glory and the resurrection of Christ, pledge of the believer's ultimate victory over death. Some private tombs in England are therefore combined with a symbolic representation of the Holy Sepulchre, at which mass was said each year at Easter time. In its earliest forms, however, tomb sculpture aimed primarily at perpetuating the funeral ceremony. It represented a festive gathering—the living assembled to pay homage to the deceased and escort him to the grave, or the priests ritually preparing the body for its eventual resurrection. Here the recumbent effigy of the dead man was the central figure on the decorated tomb, on which he lay in state till the end of time, surrounded by all the attributes of his temporal power. Here he reposed in peace—though in fact in many English tomb effigies the recumbent body appears to twitch and quiver, as if the will to live were too strong to be overborne. On the sides of sarcophagi, or those of the niche (often in the form of a chapel) in the wall of the church in which the tomb was recessed, Spanish sculptors were doubtless the first to represent the funeral procession. Assembled round the effigy of the Archbishop of Saragossa Lope Fernandez de Luna (who died in 1382), in his funerary chapel dedicated to the archangel Michael, are the twenty-four priests and monks who administered absolution, together with his three suffragan bishops and twelve of his noble kinsmen, all dressed in mourning.

In Central Italy the new sculpture was already voicing, in the accents of ancient Rome, the majestic spirit of the city republics. Its effect on the decoration of tombs was soon felt. In the church of San Domenico at Orvieto, on a sarcophagus discreetly inlaid with Cosmatesque designs, Arnolfo di Cambio carved for Cardinal Guillaume de Braye in the 1280s the first recumbent tomb effigy to appear in Italy. The monument is given, however, the characteristically Italian form of an arch of triumph. It rises up in tiers, like a series of stage-settings, and in one of the upper niches Arnolfo placed a second effigy of the Cardinal, now raised from the dead and kneeling beside his patron saints, who are commending him to the Virgin enthroned in the niche above. In Pisa Cathedral, for the tomb of the Emperor Henry VII, Tino di Camaino chose a similar arrangement, while modifying it in such a way as to exalt the earthly glory of the Emperor and emphasize the concept of Empire itself. His figure of the risen Emperor is neither kneeling nor bowed in prayer: he is shown seated on his throne, as in life, surrounded by his counsellors.

At Naples, in the church of Santa Chiara, Tino executed for the Angevin kings a whole series of funeral monuments, culminating in 1343 in the imposing mausoleum of Robert the Wise. The recess in which the tomb stands is curtained like a baldachin and designed like the portal of a cathedral. Here are a host of figures, prophets, apostles, sibyls and saints of the Franciscan Order, all assembled round the culminating scene of Christ in Glory. More explicit tribute is paid on the side of the sarcophagus to the royal power of the House of Anjou: the dead king himself is enthroned in the center, flanked by the younger members of the family who will reign after him and maintain the glory of his race. King Robert is portrayed three times. He lies barefoot in the rough homespun which, as a Franciscan tertiary, he put on to die in; this is the image of humility. He is attended however by personifications of the seven liberal arts, for well before Charles V of France the Angevin king of Naples conceived of his earthly rule as the dominion of wisdom. On the dais above the tomb effigy, Robert sits enthroned; he has joined the Caesars in the immortality of civic triumphs. Above the dais Robert lives again, this time in the eternal abode of the devout Christian, praying to the Virgin and commended by his patron saints Francis and Clare. Here the funeral decoration conveys a dual message, political and spiritual. It becomes a simultaneous expression of proud glory and pious hope. The monument keeps alive the memory of a human achievement; at the same time, it extols the virtues of renunciation and proclaims an abiding faith in the powers of mediation vested in the Virgin and saints.

But at the beginning of the fifteenth century, in response to the new mood that had cast its pall over religious observances, another aspect of death appeared on tombs—its tragic aspect, calculated to induce loathing, fear and, in consequence, contempt for the weakness of the flesh. Cardinal de Lagrange, who died in 1402, had himself represented on his tomb as a decaying corpse, while for a patrician of Florence Masaccio painted, not the body, but the bare skeleton which, in Northern Europe, was already being swept up in the eerie round of the *danse macabre*.

HEROES ON HORSEBACK

During the fourteenth century nearly every city in Italy bowed its neck to a tyrant. Either he ruled by force or the "seigniory" was conferred upon him by patrician families who, weary of ceaseless vendettas, conspiracies and tumult, hoped that the firm hand of a dictator might restore prosperity by imposing law and order.

Most of these jumped-up potentates, great and small, owed their success to the discipline and valor of the bands of mercenary troops which they employed; but they fondly imagined themselves "an antique Roman rather than a Dane," and expected their virtues to echo down the arches of the years. Nowhere in those times was a man's fame more loudly trumpeted than by the humanists in his pay who sang his praises and glorified his deeds in classical strains.

Verona and Milan were governed by men of ancient lineage and murderous temper. They lived like princes, drunk with absolute power, violent, greedy and shrewd. They were mighty hunters and renowned horsemen on the field of battle. Seeking to buttress their power by aping the deeds of the Paladins, they would come forth arrayed in the armor of Roland or Lancelot, cutting a brilliant figure at the head of their splendidly equipped companies of youthful knights as they rode out to tilt in tournaments or set off with fanfare on some campaign.

Yet they were still so insecure that they dare not perish, lest others should take their place. The usurper's act would not be forgotten in one generation, and the dead tyrant must therefore be transformed into a hero. At Verona, when a Scaliger died, his sons at first suppressed the fact, then erected his sarcophagus in the center of the town, in full view of the cowed inhabitants. Above the tomb an equestrian statue of the dead man symbolized his triumphant reign. Thus for all time Can Grande della Scala would gallop through the lists or ride in pursuit of a defeated enemy. At Milan, behind the high altar of San Giovanni in Conca, Bernabò Visconti stood motionless in his stirrups astride a great charger, unadorned and escorted only by figures symbolic of his alleged virtues. He had not crossed the threshold of death in order to kneel humbly at the gates of Paradise, but to remain a warrior and master of his city.

BONINO DA CAMPIONE (ACTIVE 1357-1388). MARBLE TOMB OF BERNABÒ VISCONTI, 1370. MUSEO DEL CASTELLO SFORZESCO, MILAN.

FUNERAL MONUMENT OF CAN GRANDE DELLA SCALA, 1329. MUSEO DI CASTELVECCHIO, VERONA.

PORTRAITS

In the early Middle Ages the few gold coins to be found in circulation in Western Europe were stamped on one side with the head of the Byzantine emperor, a privilege he alone enjoyed as sovereign and leader of the Christian world. Frederick II in the thirteenth century was the first of the Western emperors to resume this right; he made full use of it and his fame was spread abroad by his gold "Augustales."

By the fourteenth century gold currency had become much commoner. It was the normal medium of trade, being minted by the principal banking and commercial cities of Italy, such as Florence and Genoa, and to some extent by kings. Such instruments of commerce and taxation, however, never bore the likeness of a prince. The human profile only appeared on medallions, which towards the end of the fourteenth century became collector's pieces. The older dies were much sought after by connoisseurs, who would then have them copied by their own artists. The treasury of Jean de Berry contained a superb collection of coins and medallions, all stamped, not with his own features, but with those of Roman emperors. As for the medallists of the French Court, they considered only the heroes of antiquity to be worthy of their art.

Once again the wind of change blew from Italy. Petty tyrants, political freebooters and the insignificant princelings of rocky Liguria and the Apennines sought every possible means of strengthening an authority that was continually threatened by conspiracy and the condottieri. *It was they who first ventured to substitute their own profile for those of emperors or deities, and they commissioned the best artists to depict their true likeness in gold.*

Painted portraits, like medallions, were symbols of majesty and pride. At first these portraits were confined to kings, and were generally executed in profile. Before long, however, members of the royal entourage, the family, friends and favorites of the king, and even some of the more prominent businessmen who had attracted his favorable notice, began to have themselves portrayed by painters in imperial attitudes.

ANTONIO PISANELLO (1395-ABOUT 1455). FOUR BRONZE MEDALS. MUSEO NAZIONALE (BARGELLO), FLORENCE.
UPPER LEFT: SIGISMONDO PANDOLFO MALATESTA, LORD OF RIMINI (1417-1468).
UPPER RIGHT: FILIPPO MARIA VISCONTI, THIRD DUKE OF MILAN (1391-1447).
LOWER LEFT: JOHN VII PALAEOLOGUS, EMPEROR OF THE EAST (1390-1448).
LOWER RIGHT: DOMENICO MALATESTA, MALATESTA NOVELLO, LORD OF CESENA (1418-1465).

JAN VAN EYCK (1385/90-1441). PORTRAIT OF GIOVANNI ARNOLFINI, ABOUT 1434.
STAATLICHE MUSEEN, BERLIN-DAHLEM.

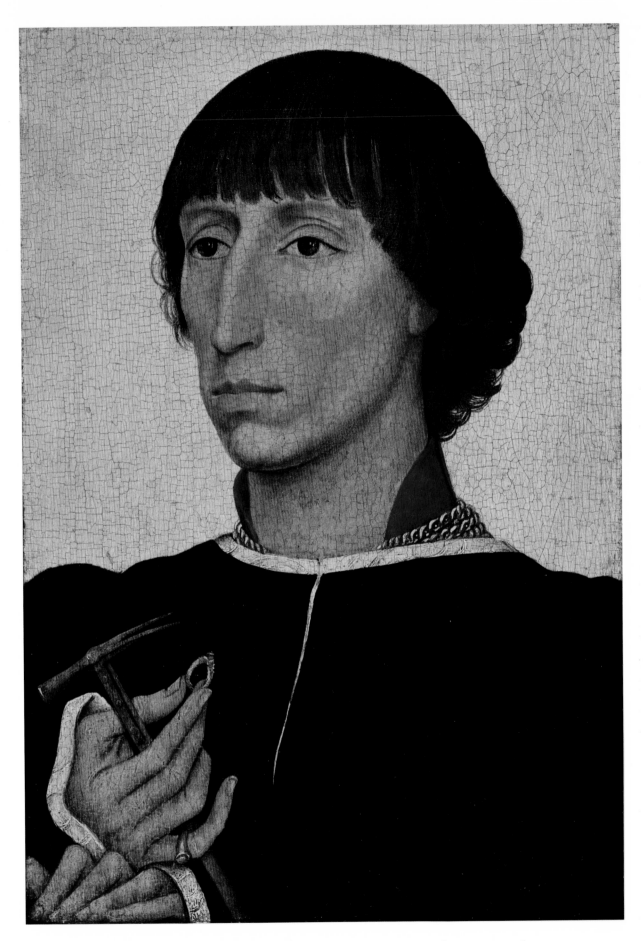

ROGER VAN DER WEYDEN (1399-1464). PORTRAIT OF FRANCESCO D'ESTE, ABOUT 1460.
THE METROPOLITAN MUSEUM OF ART, NEW YORK. THE MICHAEL FRIEDSAM COLLECTION, 1931.

141

4

THE PORTRAIT

A tomb is a personal possession. In the fourteenth
century many a rich patron of the arts thought fit
to impose on his sepulchre—as on his chapel, his
armor and his home—a visible token of himself,
in order to perpetuate his memory. For he thus made
sure that throughout the ages all who came to pray
beside his tomb would be reminded of the man he
was. And since heraldic emblems, common to a
whole lineage, did not seem to him sufficient for
that purpose, he commissioned sculptors to make
a real likeness of his face. Perhaps he also nursed
a secret hope that by so doing he was neutralizing
the dire processes of physical decay and ensuring
his survival.

The idealization of the faces of thirteenth-century
tomb effigies shows that this survival was to take
place in the world beyond the grave, following on
a glorious resurrection. The cathedral sculptures
had represented bodies unsullied by the infirmities
of their earthly lot, bodies in the prime of life and
bearing the aspect in which, according to the teaching
of the Church, they were to rise from their graves,
summoned by the trumpet and bathed in the
effulgence of the celestial light. But these abstractions had ceased to satisfy the man of the fourteenth
century; he wanted to be recognizable. When he
had his tomb built before his death, he posed for
the sculptor and insisted on a good likeness. When

the sculptor had to make an effigy of a man *post mortem*, he took guidance from the death-mask exhibited during the funeral procession. At Naples the artists commissioned to represent King Robert the Wise alive and seated on his throne made a plaster cast of the dead king's face and contented themselves with opening the eyes. The result was a terrifying effigy with a distraught gaze, that of a man roused from a nightmare and oddly resembling the wild-eyed Christ of the early Romanesque carvings.

Frankly expressionist, the art of the funerary portrait soon achieved an extreme verisimilitude. This can be seen in the recumbent tomb effigies of Wolfhart von Rot, bishop of Augsburg, Friedrich von Hohenlohe in Bamberg Cathedral and the Black Prince in Canterbury Cathedral. Son of Edward III of England, the Black Prince had come to be regarded throughout the western world, after his capture of the King of France at the Battle of Poitiers and his massacre of the inhabitants of Limoges in 1370, as the very incarnation of ruthless efficiency in warfare. The harshness and rude vigor of the carving match the personality of this grim warrior. The same style of carving serves to celebrate the pomp and power of the prince bishops and the prowess of dead knights. When, however, the sculptors were called upon to make the effigy of a dead woman, they employed a more elegant and appealing style, bringing out her physical attractions. Thus on the family tomb in Beverley Minster the face of Lady Percy, enshrined in an architectural setting "of imagination all compact," is invested with all the graces of courtly life. Cherubs bearing garlands hover round the recumbent body of the young wife of the tyrant of Lucca, Ilaria del Carretto, whose flawless beauty is immortalized by the art of Jacopo della Quercia.

When in the thirteenth century there was a revival of large-scale political statuary in Italy, the effigies of princes figured not above their dead bodies but on triumphal monuments. The earlier statues are still abstractions, not personal likenesses. The Emperor Frederick II and his chancellor Pietro della Vigna were portrayed at Capua with the features of Tiberius and Caracalla; the heroic symbolism of Roman busts was felt to be appropriate to such commanding figures, who had taken their place in history. But by the second half of the fourteenth century the old Empire was no more than a fading dream; Western Europe had been broken up into separate States and each ruler meant to be master in his own house. The attributes of supreme authority, like so many other cultural values, became vulgarized. Every European potentate desired to have his image made in painted stone, as the Emperor Frederick or Pope Boniface VIII had done before him. For he of course saw himself as the equal of these and meant to bequeath to posterity a lasting memorial of his reign. But he also wanted his features to be recognized in after times. For this purpose artists adapted the figures of cathedral sculpture, where Christ had long been represented as a king; indeed there was by now a tendency to clothe the bodies of Christ and the apostles in rich attire better suited to a social function, to show them in familiar attitudes and, generally speaking, to bring them down to the human level. All the sculptor had to do was to replace the face of a prince of the celestial hierarchy with the features of the earthly prince, his patron. Figures of this kind adorned the palaces and were often set up on the façades of churches. Philip the Bold of Burgundy commissioned from Claus Sluter a statue of himself in the attitude of prayer for the portal of the Charterhouse of Champmol; at Vienna an effigy of Duke Albert II of Habsburg, carved between 1360 and 1380, was placed in a triangular shrine at the top of one of the towers of St Stephen's Cathedral.

The new type of statuary made it easy for kings in stone to forgather with the prophets, now that the latter had almost entirely lost their aura of sanctity. Their wives, however, could not so easily mingle with the processions of female saints. For the growing spirituality of the cult of Mary then in the ascendant tended to preserve a greater distance between figures of the Virgin and those of ordinary women. The artist who carved the effigy of the French queen, Elizabeth of Bavaria, rigorously excluded any suggestion of the supramundane. The perfection at which he aimed was concerned with the beauty of the flesh alone; indeed this statue could be described as an apotheosis of the eternal feminine.

III

POSSESSION OF THIS WORLD

THE MYTHS OF CHIVALRY

The horseman on Lombard tombs, clad in armor and rejoicing in his victories, took his place among the heroes. He joined the nine Paladins whom society had chosen to symbolize its virtues and love of life; Joshua, David and Judas Maccabeus; Hector, Alexander, and Caesar; Arthur, Charlemagne and Godefroi de Bouillon. These nine paragons had been painted by Giotto in the royal palace at Naples; they had figured in tapestries woven for princes; and about 1400 their statues formed part of the new décor in noble residences. All had been immortalized by history; the first trio by the sacred history of the Old Testament; the second by ancient history, now being revealed thanks to the vogue for translations of Latin literature; the third by history that had emerged in the form of a patchwork of incidents recorded in the *chansons de geste* and in the romances of the *matière de France* and the *matière de Bretagne*. The nine Paladins clearly reveal the foundations of chivalry. While some of its heroes were borrowed from the Church, the greater part had a secular origin. Rome lay in the center, with Jerusalem to the east and Aix-la-Chapelle, *douce France* and Windsor to the West. In the background were visions of Empire, of Crusading and the Orient. There was not a priest or a saint among them. These were men of the sword, kings and warriors victorious on the field of honor. They stood for might and valor. To portray the other face of chivalry, they were accompanied by nine Heroines, embodying the spirit of gallantry. They, too, came in groups of three from the Bible, from ancient history and from courtly love.

In the lives of the men and women whose love of pomp and pleasure is depicted in fourteenth-century art, imitation of the nine Paladins and their Ladies was a natural counterpart to the imitation of Jesus Christ. The deeds of the heroes should be re-enacted in life, just as those of the Saviour should be re-enacted in the anguished hour of death. Their exemplary conduct was exhaustively described in a mass of literary effusions, besides being portrayed symbolically at festivals and ceremonies. These mimes, however, never found their way into the theater, though they were often performed effectively as side-shows to entertain the company between the courses of a banquet. Their main setting was the absorbing ritual of the new orders of chivalry.

In 1344 the victorious King of England, Edward III, under the spell of the lengthy *Roman de Perceforest*, appropriated the project of his rival in courtliness, John Duke of Normandy, the future King of France. Froissart relates how "he formed the intention of rebuilding the great castle at Windsor, originally founded by King Arthur. This had been the birthplace of the mighty Round Table, whence so many valiant men had gone forth to perform heroic feats of arms. The King decided to create an order of knighthood comprising himself, his sons and the bravest men in the land. Forty in all, they would be called Knights of the Blue Garter. Every year on St George's Day they would hold a solemn festival at Windsor. The King of England began by summoning all his earls, barons and knights, telling them of his plan and his eagerness to institute such a festival. All agreed joyously, for they believed it would be fruitful of honor and love. Then they elected forty knights who were considered by esteem and renown to excel all the others in gallantry. To the King they swore an oath to maintain the Festival and the Order in the manner prescribed. The King built St George's Chapel at Windsor Castle and appointed a chapter, lavishly endowed in cash and kind, for the service of God. In order that the Festival should be made known in every land, the King of England sent his heralds to proclaim it in France, Scotland and Burgundy, in Hainault, Flanders, Brabant and the German Empire. To all knights and squires who attended it he granted a safe-conduct for two weeks after the Festival. The forty knights and their squires were to joust against all comers. The Queen of England would be present, attended by three hundred ladies and maidens, all of noble birth and similarly attired." This was to be a closed brotherhood, headed by the King, its members chosen for their valor and congregating, like all fraternities at that time, in a chapel. Their spiritual patron, St George, was the hero of victorious jousting, and their oath bound them to practise certain virtues for the rest of their days. They had a special robe, an emblem of valor, a motto and a yearly festival on the day of their patron saint, when the renown of their champions was celebrated in the presence of ladies. Thus the new secular liturgy was developed in a setting borrowed from the devotional societies. Courtly romance and skill in worldly pursuits took the place of Lauds and mortification of the flesh. The new orders of chivalry closely imitated the fraternities of *Laudesi* in trying to portray and vindicate a rule of conduct by means of regular communal performances. They, too, resorted to imagery in the form of charades and pictures. The rules of their code, moreover, were not confined to the closed circles surrounding kings and princes. They provided a way of life for all those who aspired to enter the nobility, or at least to be considered gentlefolk. Gentility means being of good birth, and it behove those who were not born to the purple, such as captains who had won lustre in battle or citizens who had made good, to excel in knightly conduct and courtliness. Patrons of the arts were drawn from the ranks of the well-to-do, who were constrained to believe the myths of chivalry and practise its observances in everyday life. In fourteenth-century art, therefore, the imagery of courtliness forms a pendant to that of worship.

Like the "Poor Man's Bible," the *Artes moriendi* or the frescoed chapels, these images served as moral examples and precepts. Their three main themes corresponded to the three facets of knightly delectation. Most of the innumerable tapestries commissioned by Charles V of France and his brothers depicted religious scenes and were hung in chapels. The remainder comprised, firstly, pictures of the tented field or the tiltyard; Hector before the walls of Troy, the battle of Cocherel or the jousting of Saint-Denis. In the words of the *Songe du Verger*: "The knights of our time cause battles on foot and horseback to be painted in their halls, so that *by way of fantasy* they may take delight in *battles of the imagination*." Was it not the first calling and duty of a nobleman to fight in a good cause? A man of gentle birth, restrained by the code of honor, could find in battle an outlet for his combative spirit. A second feature of most secular tapestries was "verdure," whereby they obliterated the stone walls of a chamber and gave it "the fair and open face of heaven." The heroes of chivalry were also men of the countryside. They galloped through flowery meads, a sprig of may in their hand. If they started a hare, they would forsake fighting for the chase. Just as every romance was inevitably set amid the mystery and magic of a forest, so it was in the orchard that the nobleman loved to dally in his hours of ease. Lastly, there was the theme of courtly love. Around the year 1400, tapestries depicting the "Triumph of Love," the "Chamber of Love" or the "Goddess of Love," were ordered by various princes from the weavers of Paris, Arras or Mantua. They all extolled the stately concupiscence which rounded off the code of chivalry.

To these three sovereign values, all inspired by conquest—the joy of fighting, the joy of hunting, and the joy of wooing—there was added a fourth: the joy of amassing and possessing. It originated in the social upheaval which improved the status of businessmen and gradually admitted parvenus to the aristocracy. Its emergence was slow, furtive and unavowed; for chivalry took pride in being open-handed, magnificent and prodigal, and it poured scorn on stinginess. Nonetheless, secular morals were gradually tinged with gratification at one's own prosperity. This attitude first became apparent among upper-class townsfolk in Central Italy, where it conflicted with the Mendicant Friars' exhortations to poverty. Giotto is said to have written a scathing poem against those who preached abstinence, in which he substituted for complete destitution the ideal of balance and moderation. In the chapel at Padua, decorated for a man who had made a fortune in banking, the supreme Virtue, and the only one to be given a crown, is in fact Justice, namely the fair distribution of wealth. It is true that Petrarch applauded the austerity of Republican Rome, as did Boccaccio the unworldliness advocated by the Stoics he admired. It is true that the Mendicant Order of Jesuati was founded in 1360 by Giovanni Colombini, a Sienese businessman who had given all he had to the poor, and that the Florentines always turned in worship to Santa Croce or Santa Maria Novella, their two Mendicant churches. The princes of France, likewise, revered the strict poverty of the Celestines and Carthusians. By the end of the century, however, the Dominican, Giovanni Dominici, was beginning to make wealth respectable, by representing it as a condition to which some men might legitimately attain through the grace of God. He thus bestowed the accolade of the Church Predicant in rich cities on one Leonardo Bruni, secretary to the Florentine Republic, who invoked Cicero's *Tusculan Disputations* and Xenophon's *Oeconomicus* to support his contention that a man might surely acquire virtue by making money, so long as he earned it himself.

The secular ethic of enjoyment, with the concomitant pride in affluence that underlay its pursuit of pleasure, put a premium on all the good things of life that a man must leave at the end. Its values conflicted inexorably with those of piety, and their triumph in the fourteenth century showed that all the Church's efforts to christianize them had been in vain. It was all very well to portray affluence as the Lord's bounty or to affiliate a canonry to some company of knights and bestow blessings on their war-horses; it was all very well to point out that the beauties of nature merely reflected their Creator, or try to elevate a man's love for his lady into love of God. The upshot of all this was merely to give the proclivities of the age a veneer which in no way disguised their charms. The Church, in fact, surrendered to the irresistible influx of hedonism into a civilization that was becoming wholly secular. It was an age when the goldsmith's craft, at the behest not of bishops but of princes, reached new heights of magnificence. Its art, like that of the Carolingians, may be said to have been consummated in jewelry. For Suger, who loved precious stones, they enshrined the light of God and gave a foretaste of the true splendor that was to come, at present but dimly seen, and only to be unveiled on the Last Day. In the firm grasp of Jean de Berry, however, or of his cousin, Duke Gian Galeazzo Visconti of Milan, the jewel connoted earthly felicity, to be relished in all its fullness.

ARNOLFO DI CAMBIO (ABOUT 1245-1302?). STATUE OF CHARLES I OF ANJOU, KING OF SICILY, 1277. MUSEI CAPITOLINI, ROME.

POMP AND PLEASURE

In 1310 the court poet Jacques de Longuyon composed the elaborate Vœux du Paon *in which he described the procession of the nine Paladins. According to Froissart they became the exemplar for every knight or squire who aspired to win fame by feats of arms. Just as the saints had fought the good fight of repentance and salvation, so these champions in armor became the heroes of knightly legend. Fashionable society modeled itself on the valor and "gentillesse" of the Paladin, whose deeds were evoked in mime and symbol. Jean, Duc de Berry, caused the nine heroes, whose statues already adorned one of the fireplaces of his palace at Bourges, to be portrayed in a series of hangings. By means of the lacy foliation of an architectural design, the tapestry conjures up an illimitable forest, through which scenes of music and merrymaking can be glimpsed at different levels. Julius Caesar is seated on the Imperial throne; with his crown, his plate-armor and flowing Carolingian beard, he belongs to no age but is endowed with the timelessness of courtly pageant.*

History itself became a succession of warlike pageants. In battle men obeyed the rules of the tourney, and their tourneys often ended in battles. The knight went to war "neat and trimly dressed, fresh as a bridegroom," and after victory he would wait at table on his captives. Courtly art had no difficulty in combining reality with the supernatural. Every kind of painting served to show what men and women wore: scenes of coronations or illustrations for romances and love lyrics; religious subjects such as the Annunciation or, of course, the Adoration of the Magi, or even the Virgin of Sorrows. The aesthetic of chivalry required that not only its own legendary heroes but also Mary and the saints should be robed with a splendor once reserved for the most solemn rites of kingship and religion. This festal art consisted above all in shedding humdrum garments and clothing oneself in the raiment of fantasy.

After the close of the thirteenth century the new fashion began to appear in cathedral sculpture. At Strasbourg both the Tempter and the virgins he is about to lead astray are tickled by worldly pleasure. True, it is condemned by the artist, who covers the Tempter's cloak with slimy reptiles and gives the Foolish Virgins a somewhat wanton elegance. But the elegance is there, faithfully portrayed in all its lustrous charm.

NICOLAS BATAILLE (?). JULIUS CAESAR, DETAIL OF THE TAPESTRY OF THE NINE PALADINS, ABOUT 1385.
THE METROPOLITAN MUSEUM OF ART, NEW YORK. THE CLOISTERS COLLECTION, GIFT OF JOHN D. ROCKEFELLER, JR., 1947.

THE BLEST IN PARADISE. SCULPTURE ON THE TYMPANUM OF THE MAIN DOORWAY OF LEÓN CATHEDRAL, LATE 13TH CENTURY.

IVORY WRITING TABLETS REPRESENTING CHILDREN PLAYING AT HOT COCKLES, ABOUT 1375-1380. LOUVRE, PARIS.

THE TEMPTER, TWO FOOLISH VIRGINS AND A WISE VIRGIN,
ABOUT 1280. STATUES FROM THE FAÇADE OF STRASBOURG CATHEDRAL.
MUSÉE DE L'ŒUVRE NOTRE-DAME, STRASBOURG.

EROS

In the eyes of the knight and of the worthy burgess who aspired to gentility by aping him, the feast was a blazing pyre on which worldly wealth should be consumed. In feudal times pomp and extravagance had been the invariable accompaniments of government and war. The best ruler was the one who made the biggest show and shone in splendor without counting the cost. To command love and loyalty he must live in lordly style and from time to time invite all his friends to make merry with him, thus gratifying an increasingly sophisticated appetite for luxury.

Every incident in courtly life served as a pretext for a feast, and the ceremonial governing these orgies had a double purpose. Firstly, the feast was an occasion for ritual display. The lord appeared in the trappings of power and glory, laden with all the jewelry he possessed. He transferred something of his own glitter to those who had come at his bidding by presenting them with new garments. But the feast was also a ritual of destruction, a burnt-offering on the altar of hedonism. The lord solemnly sacrificed the goods painfully amassed by his toiling serfs. The junketings of the mighty mocked the poverty of the humble. By feasting the knight proved his superiority and towered contemptuously over poor drudges who labored under a heavy yoke. Let them scavenge while he caroused. By so doing he escaped the curse of Adam, condemned to eat bread in the sweat of his face. Illustrious and unconstrained, he vanquished Nature and robbed her with impunity. In death he presided at his ultimate feast, consisting in the pomp of his funeral, followed by a last banquet and a shower of gifts.

Fourteenth-century taste found its fullest expression in finery and display. Froissart's *Chronicles* were written to extol prowess, "a quality so noble and commendable that it should not be dismissed too briefly, for it is the very light and substance of a gentleman. As the log cannot burn without fire, neither can a gentleman attain perfect honor and renown without prowess." Froissart begins with a description of those sanguinary revels, the first major engagements of the Hundred Years War; he ends with the more elaborate and depraved orgies got up by Charles VI of France, who was mad. Paris in 1400 was the scene of knightly frolicking at its gaudiest. It seemed as if the spirit of carnival, in its determination to snap the bonds of daily life and escape from reality, had turned nature upside down. Darkness was banished, night and day became one and dancing went on till daybreak in the fitful, provocative gleams and shadows of torchlight. Men and women of noble birth enjoyed the freedom conferred by masks and fancy dress. In religious mimes they would act the part of the Good Thief or of Christ in agony. In dances they would become King Arthur or the wild man who slew the unicorn. And always, throughout the revels, they played at love.

The spirit of chivalry found disport in the wanton wiles of courtly love, which had beckoned the knight from the pages of every poem and romance during the past two hundred years. The clerks employed by princes had ransacked the archives of Scholasticism in order to draw up a code defining the elaborate ritual of a gentleman's relations with a high-born lady. The statutes of love appeared in the text and illustrations of books that were read aloud in the evenings to every nobleman and his household; and they were symbolized in ivory on caskets and mirrors. They were binding on any man who wanted to be received in genteel society. He must choose his Lady and serve her. Edward III of England put all the ardor and energy of youth into making himself the pattern of chivalry for his age. He was happily married. His Queen possessed all the qualities of a perfect wife and had given him two handsome children. Yet Edward went one day to the castle of the Countess of Salisbury, whose husband was his vassal, had been captured while campaigning for him and was even now held prisoner on his account. Edward wooed the lady and spent a whole evening, in the presence of her attendants, acting the part of a suitor enslaved by an invincible but hopeless love. Indeed, "Honor and Loyalty forbade him thus to perjure his heart in affronting so noble a lady and so true a knight as her husband. Yet Love spurred him so cruelly that he overcame and stifled both Honor and Loyalty." This may well have been the Lady for whom he founded the Order of the Garter, prescribed its ceremonial and chose its motto.

The ritual play of courtly love reversed the normal scheme of things. It freed a man from convention and by its essentially adulterous nature made amends for the restraints of wedlock. In feudal society marriages were contracted with an eye to the main chance. They were negotiated in cold blood and regardless of sentiment by the elders of the two clans, who concluded the bargain whereby the bride was handed over, to become her future lord's housekeeper, the mistress of his servants and the mother of his children. She had to be rich, well-born and faithful. Family law threatened with condign punishment both the adulterous wife and her would-be seducer; but it allowed the husband to fornicate and go a-whoring as he pleased. Every castle had its quota of eager damsels awaiting the knight-errant of courtly romance. This, indeed, was something more than mere dalliance, for it gave a man the option that marriage had denied him. Yet his choice never fell on a virgin, but on another man's wife. He took her not by storm but by blandishment, gradually sapping her resistance until she capitulated and granted him her favors. The whole campaign was conducted with a formal and meticulous strategy, reminiscent of the techniques employed in venery, jousting or siege warfare. Mythically, the pursuit of love became the hunt in full cry, the chosen lady a beleaguered citadel.

The knight's strategy, however, led him into bondage, for here too the normal order was reversed. In real life the lord "stoutly struts his dame before." In the game of love he must serve her, obey her lightest whim and undergo the ordeals she inflicted on him. Kneeling in adoration at her feet, in yet another reflection of the military world he adopted the posture of a vassal before his lord; for courtly language and behavior were wholly borrowed from the etiquette of vassalage. Principally there was the idea of service and all that it implied. The lover owed the same fealty to his mistress as did the liege to his lord. He had plighted his troth by an indissoluble bond. He must fight valiantly in his lady's name, for by his victories he would advance his suit. He must dance attendance on her and pay homage to her, just as feudal vassals did at their master's court. Like them, moreover, the lover expected his service to be rewarded in due time by successive gifts.

In this way the game of love sublimated and deflected sexual desire, without, however, seeking to become wholly chaste. In the thirteenth century the Church's efforts to subdue the spirit of courtliness did succeed in inspiring a number of poems which diverted the pursuit of love from a carnal to a mystic goal. This process of pious abstraction culminated about 1300 in the *dolce stil nuovo*. The ordinary swain, however, still hoped that his courtship would result in the lady's ultimate surrender, and for himself in a furtive and perilous defiance of the great taboo and of the punishment prescribed for adultery. All the same, during the period of waiting—and he was expected to wait a very long time—his lust went largely unrequited. The lover who hoped to win his lady had first to master himself. Of all the ordeals imposed by the code of love the one that best symbolized the stringency of this agreed delay was the "trial" extolled by the troubadours. The lady ordained that she and her knight should lie naked together and that he should contain his desire. Thus disciplined by the jejune pleasure of limited caresses, love would be strengthened and would attain a more emotional fervor. It would be a union of hearts rather than bodies. Thus, when Edward beheld Joan, Countess of Salisbury, he began to "ponder." Clerks in the service of feudal princes had used Ovid as a source of psychological euphemisms for physical love, and Western chivalry had adopted the code of courtliness just when Latin Christianity was being permeated with Mariolatry.

These two tendencies, making sex more spiritual and piety more feminine, intermingled and enhanced each other. Before long the Virgin became Our Lady, the paragon of her sex, to whom all men owed loving service. Her images, therefore, must be graceful, elegant and attractive. In order to captivate sinners, fourteenth-century Virgins were as exquisite in apparel and toilette as any princess. Some mystics, when they meditated upon the infant Jesus at his mother's breast, allowed their contemplation of her charms to lead them dangerously astray. Conversely, the inamorata expected her swain to voice his adoration in terms borrowed from the songs of mystic love. By becoming sentimental divine worship imparted an aura of sanctity to earthly raptures.

The fact remains that courtly love was always a game, to be played furtively with sly winks and carefully masked by a deceptive façade. It used the esoteric disguises of the *trobar clus*, of symbolic gestures and mottoes with a double meaning, of a language intelligible only to those in the know. Both in itself and in its manifestations it was, like the feast, simply a form of escapism. It was a thrilling but wholly inconsequent interlude, which no one took to heart. If those who played the game were sometimes taken in by it, they could pull themselves together by reading works that were a sort of antidote to erotic poetry. These satires and parodies, realistic and earthy, were just as popular as love lyrics. Jean de Meung's sequel to the first *Roman de la Rose*, in which his erotic allegories ended as a straightforward eulogy of physical love; the story of the Wife of Bath in *Canterbury Tales*; the bawdy anecdotes in the *Decameron*: after reading books like these a knight would drop the romantic mask and come down to earth—only to take wing again before long, for men could never decide between myth and reality. The latter, however, had no need of adornment. It was the world of feasting, illusion and romantic love that artists were expected to portray.

Courtly love was inspired and sustained by a vision. When Edward III entered the apartment of the Countess of Salisbury "everyone looked at her in wonder, and the King himself could not take his eyes from her. Then Dame Venus sent Cupid, the god of Love, to kindle the spark of passion, which burned long within him. The King, having gazed upon her, withdrew to a window, where he stood pondering deeply." Fourteenth-century art imbued clothing with poetic significance, for in order to attract attention and retain it one must make the most of one's appearance. Admission to the carnival was reserved to those whose apparel was worthy of the occasion and proved by its richness and superfluity the spendthrift extravagance of its

wearer. In the illuminations of the *Très Riches Heures* the gorgeous profusion of hoods and cloaks is almost more bizarre than the ornamental diadem of beacons blazing from the castle towers. Since carnival was part of the courtly game and consisted in a formal dialogue between the sexes, women's clothes must be sharply distinguished from men's, and in fourteenth-century courts they did in fact reach the height of feminine individuality. By accentuating sexual charms they fulfilled the purpose of erotic display. They were not particularly close-fitting but acted rather as an enticement, artfully baiting the trap of seduction. Like stained glass, whose designs and colors inspired the Parisian fashion, clothes were intended to create an illusion of unreality. In the festival women were expected, with the help of slashed and padded gowns, horned headdresses and liripipes, to quit their ordinary personality and rise above it; just as in another, mystic festival the same fashionable women, moved by the call to repentance, would hasten to burn their paraphernalia at an auto-da-fé of renunciation. Those who illuminated the margins of psalters would insert fragments of real life among the abstract flourishes of their arabesques. In the same way artists who designed dresses for courtly festivities would permit glimpses of naked flesh among the artificial trappings of their creation; for they too were aiming at a poetic illusion.

The rites of love-making, however, allowed for further visions. It was a courtly convention that the lady, as one of the tokens she bestowed on her suitor, should let him, momentarily and from afar, see her naked. Thus the lover should always be obsessed by the true image of the loved one's body. It was quite common, moreover, for women to appear naked in the *tableaux vivants* presented on occasions of State or popular rejoicing. In courtly art, on the other hand, there seems to have been a strong and enduring inhibition from painting women in the nude. This did not apply to liturgical art, but there the body was portrayed in a state of *nature* in the theological sense, that is, untainted by sin and still possessing the perfection given it by God. In cathedral sculpture these images of physical perfection occurred mainly in two settings, the Creation of man and woman and the Resurrection of the dead. In both cases the flesh is seen in glory, either before Original Sin or in the shining liberation of the Last Judgement. It is probable that about the end of the thirteenth century stone-cutters were ceasing to sculpt the body without sentiment or any recollection of pleasures they had themselves experienced. Gradually the Idea was beginning to assume physical likeness. Both Eve and those risen from the dead began to display youthful charms. The fact remains that *gula* and *voluptas*, the living flesh "mounted for the hot encounter," still cowered under the shadow of anathema or were to be seen engulfed in hell-fire. Among the devils in the Arena Chapel Giotto painted the first erotic nude in European art. It may be that others, less stricken with guilt and remorse, have disappeared. It seems, however, that throughout the fourteenth century sexual taboos remained too strong for the laity to shake them off. Women's attire at the festivities of knights and princes continued to stop short of immodesty. When sculptors or painters portrayed nudity they felt obliged to make it sinful. A certain vexation of spirit is apparent in the angular, jerky style of the *Danses macabres*, giving the figures an air of wantonness. In the Gothic world woman's body was the last of all natural forms to obtain release from sin and the fullness of earthly joy.

Here, too, Italy led the way. The legacy of Greek and Roman statuary revealed the human body free from artificial adornment, unashamedly naked.

Italian universities, emancipated from the Church, were already daring to dissect the dead, even at the risk of interfering with their resurrection. Before long sculptors began to draw inspiration from the freedom and realism of classical nudes for their own portrayal of the Creation and Last Judgement. Only at the very end of the fourteenth century did the Parisian school of painting produce a single torso with the serene innocence of antiquity and no trace of erotic sophistication; and it was that of Lazarus, a man raised from the dead. In Lombardy however, the home of chivalry, painters grew so bold as to depict Venus with nothing on, enjoying the sort of apotheosis hitherto reserved for God and the Virgin. They even showed gentlemen kneeling in adoration and receiving the spark of carnal love, much as St Francis had received the Stigmata—except that slight qualms of conscience made their hands tremble. It was not until the beginning of the fifteenth century, thanks to the patronage of Tuscan aristocrats, themselves freed by a Stoic Christianity from superstitious fear as well as from the need for erotic titillation, that woman's beauty could first be seen, after the stately Roman manner, in the perfection of bronze and marble. This was no resurrection; it was the genesis of Woman, bestowing on the New Man the gentle benison of her body.

THE BODY OF WOMAN

Among all the Virgins and saints in what we still possess of fourteenth-century art there are very few portrayals of women in the nude. Although dalliance played a large and not always clandestine part in courtly etiquette, the figure of Eve was reviled. Only when religious art depicted sin or martyrdom was it permissible to hint at worldly licentiousness.

The most vivid illustrations of lechery were at first relegated to the marginal symbols on the periphery of major compositions, where the artist had always been allowed a comparatively free hand. This was the traditional setting for parables of vice and lust, which fourteenth-century art, obedient to the Church's teaching, represented by naked women. When Parisian craftsmen carved erotic scenes in ivory on the backs of mirrors or the lids of pounce-boxes, they boldly exploited these figures, which had supposedly been placed in churches to point a moral. About 1340 one of the stone-carvers at Auxerre gave a lascivious twist to his Gothic design, resulting in the superb sculpture of a naked girl crouched against a ram in an artfully seductive pose.

Many saints endured martyrdom by torture, a theme to which the artists who recorded their lives devoted meticulous attention. Paintings of blood and lacerated flesh reflected a fairly general taste for cruelty among those who commissioned them. About 1425 Master Francke was working for devotional societies in Hamburg and Lübeck. His clients were prominent citizens who had grown rich from trade in the Baltic and the North Sea. For all their uncouthness, these men appreciated the refinement of the Parisian aristocracy and, like the big merchants from Florence and Barcelona whom they met at Bruges, they were dazzled by it. Hence the sophisticated manner adopted by the artist in relating the life of St Barbara. Her executioners are arrayed like the Magi; the scene is made more violent by the steely, twisted drawing; and the princess herself is disrobed. Piety is mingled with fashionable sadism in this virgin body exposed to the lash and the knife.

About this time Ghiberti was designing for the Baptistery in Florence the bronze door on which he depicted the creation of Woman. Here Eve is floating upwards in the arms of that flight of cherubim which hitherto had borne heavenwards only one fleshly being, the Virgin of the Assumption. This is an Eve vindicated and redeemed, rejoicing in untroubled strength. There is no executioner to menace her, no fear to make her tremble. She is numbered among the pure and blessed. Beautiful and victorious over all affliction, she soars into the light of God.

MASTER FRANCKE (FIRST HALF OF THE 15TH CENTURY). THE MARTYRDOM OF ST BARBARA,
DETAIL OF THE LEFT WING OF THE ST BARBARA ALTARPIECE, 1420-1425. NATIONAL MUSEUM OF FINLAND, HELSINKI.

PERSONIFICATION OF LUST, MID-14TH CENTURY.
SCULPTURE IN THE SOUTH TRANSEPT, AUXERRE CATHEDRAL.

LORENZO GHIBERTI (1378-1455). THE CREATION OF EVE, DETAIL OF A PANEL ON THE PORTA DEL PARADISO, 1425-1447.
GILT BRONZE. BAPTISTERY, FLORENCE.

5

GLORIFICATION OF THE FLESH

As early as the beginning of the twelfth century Provençal poets had sung of the beauties of a woman's naked body—to begin with, in a frankly ribald tone. But soon the poets of courtly love sought rather to sublimate desire, to explore the possibilities of amorous suspense, to enhance it with sensuous imaginings and gracious imagery, and to invest the body of the beloved with an almost magical glamour. A perfect work of God, summing up in herself all the splendors of creation, this very lovely lady, whether seen in the flesh or glimpsed in dreams, inspired a passionate devotion. And one of the privileges of the "very parfit knight" was to contemplate the naked beauty of his lady love. An accepted practice in the medieval courts, this rite of homage had gradually made the more cultivated knights —those who could rid themselves of the crude licentiousness of military service—more susceptible to the graces of the body. All the same, over a long period a deep-rooted inhibition told against the representation in art of a woman's physical charms. When on rare occasions, in the heyday of the troubadours, artists ventured to transpose into painting or sculpture the vision of feminine beauty which haunted the minds of the poets and their audiences, this was done so furtively, and in forms which were thought so little worthy of survival, that no trace of them remains.

Artists felt qualms about making images of *voluptas*, which could not but be suggestive. But they were allowed in images of *natura*—of bodies, that is, unblemished by sin, as God had willed them to be when He created man and woman—to represent in a less clandestine manner, for all to see, the perfection of the human form. As early as the second third of the thirteenth century, in certain monumental figurations of religious art, sculptors attempted, timidly at first, to interpret the emotions aroused by the beauties of a woman's body. Some sacred themes lent themselves to this celebration of the flesh, without offending the pious-minded. One of them was that recurrent theme of Romanesque and Gothic imagery, the Last Judgement. The scene of dead men and women rising from their graves in all the fullness of life lent itself the more readily to the artists' new aspirations since the clergy commissioning such works were themselves beginning to appreciate the pleasures of earthly life and ceasing to reject so rigorously its allurements. Already on the tympanum of Bourges Cathedral, carved in 1275, the women rising from the dead seem quickened by the joyous breath of spring, burgeoning like young flowers amid the up-ended slabs of their tombs. Here—and this was a first, decisive step towards the inclusion of purely human emotion in a sacred scene —the sculptors frankly paid homage to the elegance of well-proportioned limbs and shapely bodies. The joy that emanates from these gracious nudes is chaste; they are invested with an ethereal purity, freed from evil and the fervors of profane love.

It was the rediscovery of the long-lost remains of Greco-Roman sculpture that did most to dispel the lingering effects of the religious and social prohibitions which had led to an obsession with sin, an aversion from all that savors of the flesh and a sense of guilt wherever pleasure was involved. Towards the close of the thirteenth century, motifs from an ancient intaglio representing Hercules and Eros sleeping under a tree had been carved on the base of the portal of Auxerre Cathedral. Here we find a feeling for physical beauty quite unaffected by the Christian mistrust of it. This new interest in the human form gained ground especially in Central Italy, where throughout the Trecento sculptors and painters came under French influence. But the Italians lived in much closer contact with the works of classical antiquity. A growing interest in all that remained of ancient Rome led them to study the surviving statues and bas-reliefs and encouraged them to recapture so far as possible the spirit behind them. Already in the thirteenth century Arnolfo di Cambio's Madonnas were borrowing the stately forms of Roman matrons. Some late fourteenth-century drawings testify to a still more active and intensive study of the past. One of these, attributed to Gentile da Fabriano and now in the Louvre, represents a perfectly classical Venus, deriving from sarcophagus reliefs. But a new canon of the feminine body was developing. Though suppler and more graceful than that of the Roman marbles, it nonetheless diverged from the forms which, stemming from the aesthetic of the troubadours, had been perfected and refined in the courts of the Parisian aristocracy. Less flexible, more sensual, exempt from any qualms of conscience, it came to its full flowering in representations of the Creation of Eve on cathedral façades. The sculptor belonging to Lorenzo Maitani's workshop who decorated the façade of Orvieto Cathedral may well have worked previously on one of the great French cathedrals. He places his new-born Eve in the blithe setting of a French garden, while also giving her the strong, well-rounded forms of the ancient reliefs.

The painters patronized by the Duc de Berry successfully combined the elegant line of the Parisian artists with the graces of classical inspiration then in vogue in Italy. Thus in the scene of the paradise garden in the *Très Riches Heures* the Limbourg brothers celebrated in the lithe body of the youthful Adam and Eve's blonde beauty the joy of being alive and free in a "brave new world." In the Duke's collections there was also a medal representing Constantine the Great; on the obverse, beside a Fountain of Life surmounted by the Cross, are two figures, one of them a naked woman. The lithe, sinuous limbs, tiny breasts and supple curves reflect the mannered elegance of the Gothic courts whose highly refined art had imposed on women's bodies the fluent linearism and intricacy of the arabesque. How different from the Eve of Jacopo della Quercia, who saw her as an embodiment of strength, not of grace, a summation of the vital forces issuing from the earth, and imparted to her body the robust vigor of the goddesses of the ancient world.

POWER

Since temporal possession meant, firstly, laying down the law, fourteenth-century civilization was epitomized by the prince, whose rule conferred peace and justice. The main secular purpose of European art, largely commissioned by princes, was to glorify power, which it did in the context of feudal tradition. Power had been symbolized for centuries by the image of the armed horseman. The lord, with his prerogative of command and chastisement, was primarily a warrior who lived in the saddle. In a society where every nobleman thought himself a St George, the horse preponderated in royal art. Even in Italy, where Rome had instituted other symbols of majesty, equestrian prowess continued for a long time to be emphasized by the rumps of rearing horses, whether in the battle-pieces of Uccello or in the frescoes at the Palazzo Schifanoia in Ferrara.

From the earliest feudal times, another unmistakable image of suzerainty in its warlike pride had been the tower. The fortified citadel was not merely the base of all military operations, the rallying-point for warriors and the last center of resistance; it was also the setting for courts of justice. Flaunting its strength like a banner, the tower was above all an emblem of power. It was only lived in as an after-thought.

The same was true of the fourteenth century. Once a man reached a position of authority he erected a tower at the same time as he ordered his tomb, so that the art of princes was mainly that of building castles. When Charles V had crushed the rising under Etienne Marcel and taught the Parisians that their king would brook no restraint on his sovereignty, he built the Bastille—just as William the Conqueror had built the Tower of London three hundred years earlier. A Marquis of Ferrara constructed the so-called Rebels' Tower with stone taken from the wrecked palaces of his defeated rivals. In the calendar of the *Très Riches Heures* every

landscape forms, as it were, a jeweled setting for one of Jean de Berry's castles. These battlements also served a practical purpose. In the fourteenth century warfare was endemic and its outcome depended less on pitched battles than on capture by siege or treachery of fortresses which in fact were more important strategically than ever before. Nonetheless, it was not solely for reasons of safety that rulers held court in their castles and performed within them both their ancient, liturgical office and their newer role as intellectual patrons. The prince's chapel and library were naturally placed within the walls, whose massive strength bore witness to his authority. Thus, Charles V placed his *librairie* in a tower of the Louvre, and at Karlstein the imperial chapel was encircled by battlements. At Avignon, where French bishops now occupied the Throne of St Peter, they built a fortified palace. Its two main centers, the pontifical chapel and the hall where His Holiness sat in temporal State, were locked away behind curtain-walls. Admittedly, the gold from papal offertories had to be guarded against the constant threat of marauding bands. The fact remains that the Pope and his cardinals wanted the headquarters of their alleged paramountcy over Christendom to be designed as a stronghold. Pope Clement, however, mitigated the grimness of the battlements with a few pinnacles, and in one of the towers he had a small, elegant suite fitted up for his own use.

Fourteenth-century princes were prepared to let a certain amount of cheerfulness break into the citadel of their might. This they did in two ways. If their home was to be a castle, let it at least be a comfortable one. Ever since the twelfth century the increasing part played by women in the world of rank and fashion had been gradually weaning their menfolk from the uncouth rusticity of fighting and hunting. As a result, they no longer wore armor all the time, and by the fourteenth century they had learned to make life agreeable indoors, even after dark and in winter, by means of torchlight and the glowing hearth. It behoved the prince, as a paragon of chivalry and "the mirror of all courtesy," to make provision in his home for the arts of conversation and love. Beside the great hall, therefore, where the men-at-arms congregated and the lord dispensed justice, newly-built or renovated castles contained a number of small apartments, to which fireplaces and tapestries added comfort and charm. It was in the fourteenth century that the prince's castle began to develop into a mansion. That of Saint-Paul, Charles V's favorite residence in Paris, had in its grounds several pavilions elegantly designed for recreation.

The second improvement was decorative. War itself was an occasion for display. It was the most stirring of all festivals, and the knight went forth to it in his bravest attire. Fourteenth-century battle-fields were strewn with gaudy surcoats, tatters of silken cloth, gold belts and a rich detritus of jewelry. The first duty of court painters was to embellish military equipment. In 1386, when the barons of France assembled in Flanders with a view to invading England, they wanted "their ships to be lavishly adorned and emblazoned with their badges." The Duke of Burgundy entrusted the decorating of his ship to his artist, Melchior Broederlam. According to Froissart, "Painters were in clover. There were not enough to go round, and they could earn whatever they asked. They made banners and standards from scarlet silk of surpassing fineness. Masts were painted from top to bottom, and some, in token of wealth and power, were covered with pure gold-leaf. Beneath was displayed the coat-of-arms of the noble to whom the ship belonged."

Since the ritual of war required all this parade of frills and furbelows, the baron's castle must also be adorned. Like his helm, it was crowned by an elaborate frieze, reproducing in stone the jeweled lattice-work of a reliquary and using the same Gothic arabesques in which the fantasy of courtliness found expression. Their convolutions reached the height of eccentricity in the roof of Jean de Berry's castle at Mehun-sur-Yèvre. Higher and higher rose these bastions and symbols of feudal power, with their banners and pennants streaming in the wind and their exuberant façades borrowed from rood-screens and the illuminations of missals, becoming in the end "such stuff as dreams are made on."

Europe, however, was beginning to embrace another concept of power, more ascetic and deriving from Roman law. Far more men were thinking about politics and the mechanics of power, largely because States themselves were growing stronger and better organized. Rulers had to employ officials of wider education, whose university training had accustomed them to reason methodically. National assemblies were convened at which representatives of the higher orders were asked to give advice on matters of State and even to debate policy. In the fourteenth century Europeans began to develop civic consciousness, and more of them were capable of conceiving power in abstract terms. About this time professional thinkers were bringing their minds to bear on the problems of government, for political science belonged to the realm of secular inquiry that William of Occam had thrown open to experiment and rational deduction. Scholars were at first preoccupied with the central conflict of medieval politics, namely, the ancient rivalry of Pope and Emperor, the twin potentates who, since the days of Charlemagne, had been dependent on each other and had both claimed to rule the world. That struggle had virtually ended in the middle of the thirteenth century with the triumph of the Holy See. But this in itself led to an argument about the origins of civil authority. While the jurists employed by the Pope used all the artillery of Scholasticism to win him a theocratic interpretation, those of Philippe le Bel, King of France, sought in Roman law the means to demolish the inordinate claims of Boniface VIII. In this they were allied to the Italian Ghibellines who, like Dante in his *De monarchia*, upheld the Holy Roman Empire. In this way the quarrel blew up again early in the fourteenth century. The transfer of the Papacy to Avignon made its worldly proclivities more apparent than ever. A German monarch invaded Italy in order to seize the imperial diadem. A large section of the Franciscan Order took issue with the Pope over the definition of poverty. At this moment two works appeared that were to inspire political philosophy throughout the fourteenth century.

When the Franciscan, William of Occam, wrote the *Dialogus*, after being prosecuted for heterodoxy by the Curia at Avignon and taking refuge with the Emperor, he continued to apply his basic principle of segregating the secular from the religious. In his rigid separation of Church and State he accorded the latter the exclusive right to political action. "The Pope," he said, "may not deprive men of liberties conferred on them by God or by nature." This enthronement of Nature beside God as a source of law implied far-reaching secularization of thought and jurisprudence. Meanwhile two professors at the University of Paris, Marsilio of Padua and Jean de Jandun, had previously published another work, *Defensor pacis*, which was far more subversive and uncompromising in the violence of its onslaught upon ecclesiastical authority. The Church had filched its temporal prerogatives from the Prince. It was wrong to suppose there could be any autonomous spiritual power, for there was no spiritual nature outside the laity. Hence, any special prerogative attaching to the Church must have been usurped and should be surrendered to the State. But how did the State obtain its authority? According to feudal tradition it was bequeathed by the sword, as a result of victorious warfare waged by the prince's ancestors. According to ecclesiastical Schoolmen it was a gift from God, who delegated His power to Kings—using, the Popes hastened to add, St Peter as His agent. The *Defensor pacis* had the downright audacity to attribute the origin of secular authority to the people, namely, "the majority of citizens who promulgate the law."

People, liberty, citizens, law, majority: such words, soon to be echoed by virtue, order, happiness, had the authentic ring of Roman maxims. Although they were still heard amid the din of war-cries, the voices were no longer those of Crusaders, but of legionaries and lictors. Marsilio of Padua gleaned them from the pages of Livy: Petrarch enriched them from his store of classical learning; and by the end of the fourteenth century Charles V of France was assuming the air of a Philosopher-King. He let it be known that he meditated in his book-room and frequented the company of scholars; that in winter "he would often read until supper-time the noble tales of Holy Writ, or the deeds of the Romans, or the moral teaching of philosophers." He had Aristotle's *Politics* translated, and the *Songe du Verger* gave him a theory of royal sovereignty wielded for the good of the *res publica* and guided by the advice of wise and moderate men. "When thou takest thy ease from the care and great thought thou givest to thy people and the common weal, then dost thou privily read or cause to be read some good writing and doctrine." The King no longer

led his army in battle but entrusted it to a High Constable. The Clerk had once more got the better of the Knight; but now he was a lay clerk, steeped in "the deeds of the Romans."

This new, civil authority, claiming to originate in nature and to rest on the people, required new emblems and symbolic figures. There was still room for the horse, provided it was that of Constantine or Marcus Aurelius, but no longer for the tower. In ancient Rome the sovereign was honored and set on a pedestal of power by other devices, whose remains Frederick II had unearthed and appropriated in Southern Italy. In the year 1300, when Pope Boniface had, by promising indulgences, lured all Christendom to the imperial and apostolic city, he caused the finest artists in Italy to place similar emblems around his throne, and he had statues of himself erected in cities that had been conquered on his behalf. The prince's power was manifested in his own lifetime by his appearance in triumphant effigy. Fourteenth-century magnates, accompanied by their household, were portrayed in majesty above the recumbent figures on their tombs, and they displaced prophets, apostles or the Queen of Sheba from the porticoes of churches. Among the first was the Emperor Henry VII whose effigy stood in the apse of Pisa Cathedral, while a little way off those of his four counsellors kept watch over his tomb. Charles V had himself portrayed, with his wife and sons, on the new staircase in the Louvre. The Kings of Bohemia stood sentinel over the Charles Bridge in Prague. Above the great fireplace in the palace at Poitiers, the lovely Queen Elizabeth of Bavaria looked down in regal distinction.

Opposite the Emperor's statue at Pisa there stood another, not of a lady but of an abstract, semi-divine power—the City herself. The city republics set out to glorify the civil attributes of power, as revealed by jurists in the laws of ancient Rome. Indeed the most advanced among them, in Central Italy, made great play with their Roman ancestry. Governed by sworn councils of citizens, who were theoretically equal and held office by turns, they pursued a martial, often aggressive policy, whose execution they entrusted to hired mercenaries. They believed law and order, on which trade and prosperity throve, to depend on internal harmony, freedom, loyalty and devotion to their city and to one another. They must unite for the greater glory of the city, which was reflected in massive buildings, constructed at public expense and designed by artists chosen competitively. Various symbols of military power survived amid these trappings of civic prestige. The campaniles of their collegiate churches stood ponderously foursquare, their façades, blank at the base, gradually becoming ornate towards the summit. These and the towering belfries of town-halls in Northern Europe had the fortified appearance of royal castles. The civic palaces of Tuscan *podestà*, those embodiments of imperial power, consisted of houses in the Roman style with inner courtyards, but transformed into fortresses and crowned by beetling towers. Moreover, every patrician family insisted on building a tower of its own. It was also thought fitting that victorious *condottieri* should be honored with statues, so that public squares and the façades of town-halls were soon teeming with feudal cavalry. In one respect, at least, this new municipal art did not favor warlike motifs. At the foot of the municipal tower public fountains gave a more peaceful air to the newly-built colonnades. Although in the last decades of the fourteenth century the loggia at Nuremberg was still adorned with the Nine Paladins of chivalry, the fountain which Nicola Pisano had constructed long before, in 1278, for the municipality of Perugia incorporated features of the new civic iconography. His patriarchs, saints, signs of the zodiac, symbols of the months and the liberal arts—all these obeyed the Scholastic traditions of the Church; but nearby he placed the She-wolf suckling Romulus and Remus, and the twin effigies of Perugia and Rome, *caput mundi*. Some years later, Labor and Good Government, the pillars of peace and order, were sculpted on the lowest tier of the campanile at Florence.

Nothing survives of the earliest Italian frescoes glorifying civic majesty, such as Giotto's horoscope of Padua, which he painted for the Palazzo Comunale in strict accordance with a plan scientifically worked out by a professor at the University. The oldest existing panegyric of this kind is that completed by Ambrogio Lorenzetti, between 1337 and 1339, on the instructions of the Republic of Siena. It is still the most consummate and expressive. The authorities had previously commissioned Simone Martini to decorate the outside of the town-hall with scenes from Roman history. To keep themselves in the path of righteousness they must also have constantly before their eyes the virtues they should practise and the consequences of their administration. It was decided to give them food for thought in the contrasting allegories of Good and Bad Government. Ambrogio was directed to provide the Council Chamber with a convincing portrayal of the Aristotelian principles enunciated by the Schoolmen. In those days the lay mind could only grasp abstract ideas through the medium of allegory. If they were to be effective they must assume the form, countenance, dress and attributes of living men. That is why fourteenth-century didactic verse is filled with such a depressing phalanx of allegorical figures. Rubbing shoulders with the saints and dressed in much the same way, they made their inevitable appearance in every mime that tried to render a concept pictorially intelligible. They likewise cluttered up a large area of secular painting.

In the Council Chamber at Siena Bad Government is portrayed by the Prince of Evil, trampling Justice underfoot and escorted by the four powers of confusion—Disorder, Avarice, Vainglory and Wrath. Against them is set the triumph of Good Government, throned in majesty and clothed with the civil attributes of a sovereign. He has the bearded countenance of an Emperor. At his feet the She-wolf is suckling Romulus and Remus, and he is guarded by a troop of knights, their lances at the ready. In his splendor he emulates the Almighty, come to judge the good and the wicked. On his left, chained and captive, are the enemies of the City, the sowers of discord whom his victory has subjugated; on his right stand the twenty-four councillors, the serene masters of good doctrine. He, like St Thomas Aquinas in his Dominican apotheosis, is advised by allegorical figures—not the Nine Paladins, but the Nine Cardinal Virtues. In the sky, dominant but remote, are the three Theological Virtues. Around and a little below his throne, like the kings who in symbolic pictures of the Empire waited upon the Vicar of God, are seated in majesty the six Virtues of earthly life: Magnanimity and Strength; Temperance, Prudence and Justice. Lastly, "Sweet Peace sits crowned with smiles." A little way off, Justice is depicted again, in full face and enthroned with the same degree of stateliness. Inspired by Wisdom, she punishes the bad, rewards the good and, by giving and taking away, makes equitable distribution of worldly goods. (The fresco, after all, was commissioned by a Seigniory dependent on the *popolo grasso*, who regarded wealth fairly earned as lawful.) From the even scales of Justice hang two ropes which Concord is braiding in token of the friendship uniting the officers of State. In this way the abstract concept is given substance.

The impact of these Virtues, however, on Siena and its countryside is felt palpably in the humdrum events of daily life. These appear below the allegory, as if on a stage. They are no longer framed symbolically in the architecture of a chapel, for politics has no truck with liturgy. A whole people is working peacefully in pursuit of legitimate wealth. By their manifold tasks, depicted in minute detail, they earn enough to secure themselves from want and attain a greater measure of social justice. In the sweat of their face, moreover, do the peasant and merchant make possible the revels and recreations of the nobility, the butterfly dancing of maidens and the gallant cavalcades of falconry. Yet what finally emerges from this allegory of civil power is one of the finest portrayals of Nature in the whole of Western art. It is the first authentic landscape.

TOWERS

The fourteenth-century aristocrat's lust for power appears in the development of military architecture. It assumes two strikingly different forms in the ornate splendor of the château of Mehun-sur-Yèvre, near Bourges, one of Duke Jean de Berry's favorite country seats, and in the severely plain, slightly menacing architecture of the towered city represented by Ambrogio Lorenzetti in his Good Government fresco at Siena. (Something of the same contrast may be seen between the late medieval church spires of the German towns and the bristling towers of early Renaissance palazzi in Italy.)

The Limbourgs' miniature and Lorenzetti's townscape speak, as it were, two different languages. One has the ethereal dimensions of courtly myth, the vertical impetus of a mystical ascension; even the two peaks behind the castle (as well as the tree on the lower right) appear to be spiraling upwards, while the composition as a whole suggests the mazy convolutions of a poetic reverie. In the other a severe pattern of plain surfaces, staggered and interlocking, delineates a world of mass, density and depth.

The two works in fact represent two civilizations. The towers of the French prince's château are each capped by a hexagonal room as richly sculptured and traceried as a fairy-tale palace; the defensive apparatus is concealed beneath a riot of festive ornament. It is a setting fit for the fabulous adventures of King Arthur's knights as they roamed enchanted forests. A symbol of knightly lavishness, it glitters with the promise of treasure to be scattered far and wide. Such treasure, however, was jealously guarded from hostile neighbors by the towers of patrician families in Siena, or by that of the municipality at Gubbio. A few loggias were provided to admit fresh air, but the main purpose of these castles and palazzi was to unite kinsmen or townsfolk in a joint enterprise of economic rivalry and conquest. They were built to beat down competition.

THE LIMBOURG BROTHERS. THE CHÂTEAU DE MEHUN-SUR-YÈVRE, ABOUT 1415.
MINIATURE FROM THE "TRÈS RICHES HEURES DU DUC DE BERRY," MS 1284, MUSÉE CONDÉ, CHANTILLY.

THE SPIRE OF ST STEPHEN'S CATHEDRAL, VIENNA.

THE SPIRE OF ULM CATHEDRAL.

THE PALAZZO DEI CONSOLI AT GUBBIO (UMBRIA).

THE DUCAL PALACE AT MANTUA (LOMBARDY).

6

THE PALACE

In the fourteenth century the days of feudal independence were over; it had succumbed to the centralizing power of the monarchs. The world had grown smaller now that the crusades had come to an end and the military exploits of the knighthood were confined to the continent of Europe. A hundred years earlier the young King Edward III of England would, like his forbear Richard Cœur de Lion, have gone to the East in quest of glory; instead, he plundered nearby France. Henceforth the taste for military adventure found an outlet in the political field, as was indeed to be expected given the European situation. Christendom was now split up into separate States—a few great kingdoms, many minor principalities, and that host of small republics, fiercely competitive and at odds with each other, constituted by the towns of Italy and Germany. Everywhere the ruling princes and municipal magistrates had to cope with the unrest due to family feuds and rival factions. The western world resounded with the clash of arms throughout a century which witnessed an amazing development in military techniques and the art of fortification. Princes and towns saw to it that they were protected by stout walls. But the function of the castle was not merely to protect; it signalized the power of the kings and nobility. When, though perhaps less well off than some of his peasant neighbors, a country squire wished to ensure their deference, he built a turret on to his house, and it was more for reasons of prestige than of defense that royal palaces, like town halls, were given the air of fortresses.

Once it was clear that they would have to prolong their stay at Avignon, the Popes decided to build a residence befitting their hegemony. Benedict XII, who had been a monk, gave orders for the building of a papal palace laid out like a monastery near Notre-Dame des Doms. A narrow, austere edifice in the Cistercian style, it was flanked by bare ramparts giving it the look of a stronghold. Clement VI enlarged the palace and added a new unit centering on an immense courtyard suitable for receptions and parades. At the top of a staircase wide enough for ceremonial processions, he opened up a large decorated arch where the Holy Father could show himself to the public on solemn occasions. One of the towers contained a private apartment equipped with comfortable rooms and adorned with frescoes. But the exterior of the palace retained a forbidding aspect, like a clenched fist. This was not only to ward off the roaming bands of freebooters whose leaders threatened that one day they would carry off the Pope's gold, but also because the Pope was determined (to the dismay of the mystics) to lord it like one of the princes of this world, and to be if possible the most powerful of them all. Like Karlstein, like the old Louvre, like Bellver Castle built for the King of Majorca, the Palace of Avignon had in the heart of the building an open space, surrounded by loggias, where festivities were held. At the same time it safeguarded the person of the Pope with a cuirass of inviolable majesty.

Most of the cities of fourteenth-century Europe were dominated by a princely castle, a perpetual reminder of the overlordship of the State. At Prague, facing the merchants' quarter, the famous bridge built by the Emperor Charles IV to connect the left bank of the Vltava with the approach to his palace on the Hradcany hill was entered by a fortified gate. Serving less for defense than to glorify the royal house, it was adorned with monumental effigies of the kings of Bohemia. Some towns, however, had succeeded in securing for themselves a partial, sometimes a complete right of self-government, and they too sought to proclaim their autonomy by erecting grandiose buildings. For a long while these were always churches, and the towns that built and adorned them at their own expense competed with each other to raise the highest spire. From generation to generation the local patricians added arcades, marble facings and pieces of sculpture, flaunting their wealth in the lavish decoration of their churches. In the churches, too, figured the first proud testimonies to the power and grandeur of the town itself. In 1310 the municipality of Pisa commissioned from Giovanni Pisano a symbolic effigy of the town. The artist gave it the form of a crowned caryatid feeding two children, as the Roman wolf had suckled Romulus and Remus. Likewise he endowed the figure with the ponderous majesty of the Roman tradition; it was upheld by the imperial eagle and escorted by the four cardinal virtues, one of them, Prudence, naked in the manner of a classical Venus. Nevertheless he placed this work in the cathedral, as one of the supports of the Gospel pulpit.

As early as the first half of the fourteenth century the free towns of Germany were financing the construction of town halls, seats of the local government, which, given the form of castles, resembled the residences of the nobility. Italian cities too were beginning to divert the sums raised by taxation from churches and chapels to public works of a purely civic nature. In 1334 Giotto was appointed city architect at Florence, superintending the work done not only on the cathedral but on the municipal palace, the Arno bridges and the city walls. The Campanile he designed belonged more to the Municipality than to the Church, and the sculptures at its base celebrated the Arts and Industries of the townsfolk.

The architecture of the city republics always contained a twofold central element: a castle and, beside it, a square. Like the kings, the local magistrates conferred in a tower overlooking an open space used for mustering the militia and for public meetings. The townsfolk of Gubbio built a handsome fortress-like *palazzo* for their consuls and, at the cost of tremendous efforts, flanked it with a lofty esplanade never used for trade or commerce. On this elevated platform, in the full glare of the Umbrian sun, the civic ceremonies took place. The people of Siena curtailed work on the huge cathedral planned by their fathers and, instead, erected in the semicircular Piazza del Campo a group of civic buildings, the first example of town planning in Christian Europe. The main unit was the Palazzo Pubblico, begun in 1298; on one side of it stands an elegant tower, the Torre del Mangia, which, despite its slenderness, served a military purpose and symbolized the city's proud intent to guard her independence.

NATURE

Despite the tramping of men-at-arms and the ravages of plague, the fourteenth century was one of the great ages of song. Its lyrics, written to be sung in gardens, told of shepherds, the countryside and spring. Girls danced to them in meadows, and the roundelay of maidens in flowered dresses brought to the stony, angular Siena of Lorenzetti something of the smiling fields beyond the walls. Zest for life found fulfilment in the pure air of woods and fields. The art it inspired brought rustic pleasures indoors, transferring them to the walls of the closet or the pages of a book, where they conjured up dreams of roaming through field and forest, or recalled the familiar smell of grass and the hunter's prey.

Chivalry had originated in a society to whom towns were almost unknown. The lord of the manor owed his prosperity to land and the peasant who tilled it. Princes were always on the move from one estate to another, and they held court in completely rural surroundings. It is well known that St Louis loved to dispense justice beneath an oak, and much of the fourteenth-century knight's fierce relish for the fray consisted in the fact that warfare was, so to speak, an open-air sport. He charged through vineyards, skirmished along the edge of forests and laid about him amid the warm fragrance of freshly-turned earth. Battles began in the dewy dawn and waxed hotter as the sun rose in the sky. The castle, too, emerging from its battlemented seclusion, prepared a garden for the gentler pursuits of courtly life. At Avignon the Pope planted an orchard within the walls of his palace. Karlstein and Windsor were far from Prague and London. In Paris, since the old palace on the Ile de la Cité and even the Louvre were too remote from green fields, Charles V bought gardens in the Marais and there built his mansion of Saint-Paul. Every well-to-do merchant, aping the nobility, wanted to live in rural ease by acquiring land outside the city walls. Although Western society was becoming more and more urban in manners, tastes and occupations, it was so obsessed by the feudal lord as the embodiment of human happiness that it also succumbed to the charms of rusticity.

It so happened that Virgil had extolled those charms long ago, and the early Humanists, having rediscovered him, began to sing the praises of bucolic life, to point out how happy shepherds were and to bid their disciples exchange the tainted luxury of courts for the joys of pastoral simplicity. Countrified retreats became the setting for leisured converse. The convivial circle of the *Decameron* did not meet within the walls of Florence, and Petrarch forsook the bustle of Avignon for the lonely pool of Vaucluse.

It even became fashionable for worship to move out of doors. The only really religious characters in courtly romances were hermits, who shared with fairies the seclusion of thick forests. The sanguine spirit of Chivalry sought and found a God "who dwelt among the untrodden ways." For the believer who should forsake ritual and aspire after perfect love, "the radiance of God," said Meister Eckhart, "is everywhere, for all things give him the savor of God and reflect His image." Mystic ecstasy would convey the soul to an orchard, walled about but filled with flowers and birds and babbling brooks. The medieval church had crowned the Virgin and had shown her to the people as a queen enthroned amid angels and the solemn pomp of power. The fourteenth century brought her back among men. She shared the grief of atonement as they lay stricken before the dead body of their God; but she also partook of a woman's happiness. Rejoicing in the Visitation, or in the Birth and Childhood of Christ, the Virgin was embowered among the same garlands that Joan of Arc and her companions hung on summer nights from the trees where fairies lived. Seated on a grassy bank, she reigned over nature at peace.

To medieval monks and priests Nature had connoted the abstract idea of a perfection that lay beyond the senses. It was the conceptual form in which God manifested Himself—neither the tenuous chimera of sight, hearing or smell, nor the phantasmagoria of the world, but Eden as it had been before the Fall. It was a universe of peace, moderation and goodness, ordered by divine reason and as yet immune to the chaos and degradation wrought by sex and death. *Natura* stood in contrast to *gula* or *voluptas*, the warped nature of man, headstrong and disobedient to God's commands, and therefore abject, contemptible and damned. Twelfth- and thirteenth-century thinkers regarded Nature as something spiritual and incorporeal, whose mystery could not be discovered by the mere observation of phenomena, but only by proceeding in thought, from one deduction and one abstraction to another, until the ultimate divine reason was attained. Medieval physics was wholly conceptual, which was why it found Aristotle so congenial.

The Stagirite, it is true, based his physics on observation; but his path of inquiry wound upwards, in a manner identical to that of Scholastic logic, from the particular and fortuitous to the general, issuing finally in a concept. In this way knowledge gradually went beyond the shifting, ephemeral appearance of things in an attempt to reach the essential bedrock of all phenomena. By successive stages of abstraction it arrived at the Aristotelian forms of physics, mathematics and metaphysics. Physics, the knowledge of what is still subject to change, was thus rigidly separated from mathematics, the knowledge of what becomes fixed when the process of abstraction reaches the point where movement ceases. Aristotelian philosophy, once it had been translated from the Arabic, was enthusiastically espoused by masters and scholars of the Arts at the University of Paris. They were carried away by this complete, systematic, wholly rational cosmology, with its symmetrical counterpart in the microcosm of man himself.

This conceptual vision of the world made it all the easier to explain Nature as the embodiment of divine reason. Since art, moreover, was dominated by men who despised the sinful lusts of the flesh and, in their pursuit of knowledge, discarded observation and experiment in favor of the syllogism and pure logic, it was inevitable that Early Gothic, like Romanesque, should be abstract rather than repre-sentational. It did not depict a tree but the idea of a tree, just as it did not depict God, who was not apparent, but the idea of God.

Yet God had made Himself flesh. During the thirteenth century ecclesiastical art gradually moved from the essence of what it portrayed to its actual appearance. Before long it was possible to identify in the stonework of capitals the leaves of lettuce, strawberry and vine. The new Christianity preached by St Francis, whose optimism was akin to that of chivalry, urged that Brother Sun and other creatures of this world should be restored to honor, and its gradual propagation did much to revive men's interest in reality. The Friars Minor were numerous and influential at the University of Paris and the court of St Louis, and they spoke appreciatively of Nature as one of the glories of God in which the eye might take delight.

Even among Schoolmen some doubts arose as to the infallibility of Aristotle. Scholastic logic had itself been devised to expose and resolve conflicts between authorities. Before long it found that the Aristotelian cosmology did not quite agree with other systems, such as that of Ptolemy, revealed by translations of the *Almagest*. Only physical observation could eliminate these discrepancies and adjudicate between contradictory opinions. In the thirteenth century astronomers at Merton College, Oxford and at Paris University became the first Western scholars to make deliberate use of experimental method.

A more serious objection to Aristotelian physics was that it conflicted with Christian dogma. By imprisoning man in the cosmos it denied him free-will, and by postulating the indestructibility of matter it left no room for the Creation or the Crack of Doom. The exposition of Averroes made it brutally evident where peripatetic physics flew in the face of Christianity. In 1277, therefore, they were both solemnly condemned by Etienne Tempier, Bishop of Paris. This piece of intellectual tyranny had the effect of emancipating Western thought. By discarding a comfortable system which had an answer for everything, it plunged the world back into mystery and made scholars think for themselves.

Already the Franciscans at Oxford were beginning to blaze new trails. When Robert Grosseteste gain-said Aristotle by his hypothesis that the substance common to the whole universe was light, man's concept of it was no longer "cabined, cribbed, confined," but flung open to the infinite. Since light could itself have been lit and might one day go out, one could imagine the world as having a beginning and an end. The new system, moreover, implied some form of calculus. Once the universe was interpreted in terms of light, physical reality could only be investigated by means of optical laws, which themselves were dependent on geometry and arithmetic. Mathematics were once more allied to physics and there was a strong inducement to calculate the size of the earth. The mystical tradition of numbers handed down by the Neo-Platonists could be harnessed to the new cosmogony.

As a result, exact science began to make rapid strides after the year 1280. According to Aristotle, the four elements were wholly abstract. The scholars of Oxford and Paris now sought to make them quantitative. Owing to the theory of light, implying scintillation, dynamism and thrust, the stable mathematics of the Greeks gave way to a mathematics of flux. Finally, the new doctrine illuminated the whole realm of knowledge by laying fresh emphasis on visual observation and giving it pride of place among methods of research.

At the end of the thirteenth century the vacuum created by the repudiation of Aristotle was filled when another Oxford Franciscan, William of Occam, convinced the Schoolmen that all abstract knowledge was illusory and that man's intellect could not penetrate the mystery of matter, which could only be apprehended sensorially in its external and fortuitous aspects. He thus restored the paramount importance of what men can touch and see. Thanks to the intellectual tide that reached the flood in Occamism and swept through the fourteenth century, the abstract in nature became concrete and things were once more what they seemed. This, combined with Franciscan joy and courtly exuberance, encouraged artists to open their eyes and behold "the many-splendored thing."

The world of chivalry, which now superseded the Church as patron of the arts, was inquisitive by nature and loved to see strange or exotic sights that gave free rein to fantasy. The knight-errant was by definition a vagrant and by predilection an explorer. The Crusades had furnished a pretext for travel on the grand scale, and few crusaders had been indifferent to the tourist attractions of the Levant. When books came to be written for this type of reader, they were mostly concerned with distant countries. Even in the early *chansons de geste* the pine and the olive stood as symbols for the recollection of bygone journeys and the yearning to set off once more. Tales of genuine travel competed with romances about knightly adventures in a world of myth and imagination. *Bestiaries, Lapidaries, Mirrors of the World, Wonder Books, Tales of Treasure Trove*: works like these, written in the vernacular for the courtiers of great noblemen, gave detailed descriptions of strange creatures which, unlike the unicorns and dragons, really existed. Every fourteenth-century ruler, partly for amusement but also because he wanted to possess the whole world, built up collections of curios which traders brought from the ends of the earth. In his gardens he kept a menagerie where live monkeys and leopards were on view.

There was also much speculation about the more humdrum aspects of nature, which nonetheless had their mystery and gave scope for fascinating discoveries. Hunting was in itself a form of conquest, for it enabled men in their daily lives to seize and subjugate the humbler creation. By means of the chase they became closely and accurately acquainted with the behavior and habitat of wild animals. Some of them, beginning with the Emperor Frederick II, embodied their experience in treatises. Together with love lyrics and chronicles of exploration, books on venery were among the earliest literary products of the knightly caste. They were the first writings on natural history, and they enjoyed a tremendous vogue. People were delighted when animals or plants they had observed in the hunting-field reappeared along the margins of their psalters or breviaries. Artists depicted them alongside fabulous beasts or wreathed in the trailing arabesques of imaginary flowers.

Taste in the age of chivalry required the portrayal of objects to be realistic but discrete, so that they should be individually identifiable and at the same time secluded and deeply interwoven with memory or poetic vision. The aristocracy made no attempt to display the whole pageant of nature: they merely selected a number of isolated features which were dotted about ornamentally amid the embroidered curlicues of their tapestries. These natural objects were pricked out against the abstract setting, such as a gold background or the red-and-blue checkerboard of stained glass, which was usually employed for ceremonial purposes.

Occamist physics had replaced the logical unity of a conceptual universe by a world consisting of disparate phenomena. Having destroyed the fullness and solidity of Aristotelian space, the Occamists had filled the vacuum with a gallimaufry of collector's pieces, which they tried to co-ordinate by means of the *impetus* or life-force, for which the Parisian scholar Buridan devised a mathematical rationale. Its movement resembled the swirling of the dancers' garlands in a roundelay, or the eddying of caparisoned horses in the vortex of the tiltyard. Although the Oxford scholars founded the science of optics, it was not from them that painters learned the laws of perspective. Nature as portrayed in the joyous art of chivalry had none of the structural solidity, based on mathematics, of the Romanesque basilica or Gothic cathedral. Spatially, it consisted in a series of piercingly vivid but unco-ordinated glimpses. The first attempts at constructing a landscape in paint were made in Italy.

Here the militant Franciscans extolled poverty of spirit and fulminated against scientific inquiry. Consequently the universities remained generally impervious to Occamism and continued to expound Aristotle and Averroes. The old philosophy lingered on until the teaching of Plato burst upon Florence with belated but devastating effect.

In the Italy of the fourteenth century, with the exception of medicine, all scientific achievements came from abroad. The intelligentsia consisted for the most part of bishops and Preaching Friars, who educated the upper classes and determined the iconography used in decoration. They retained the image of a unified, conceptual and wholly co-ordinated universe. Yet it was Italian artists, returning to the fountain-head of classical painting, who first rediscovered the ancient methods of creating illusion. Both the stately performances of civic ceremonial and those portraying the life of Jesus required no more than purely symbolic scenery and a few simple indications of time and place. They had therefore used the same abstract idiom as Roman or Byzantine art. The characters were surrounded by stylized trees and rocks, buildings and thrones. On the other hand, it was inherent in the dramatic quality of this art that the scenery should be arranged intelligibly within an enclosed space, and that the unreality of the setting should not clash too violently with the flesh-and-blood authenticity of the actors. On Giotto's majestic stage God and the saints were firmly delineated with all the massiveness and physical reality of statues. They had therefore to be given a certain amount of elbow-room. Giotto made no attempt to surround them with atmosphere or to pierce the wall behind them with a receding vista; but he did try, by means of a rather labored perspective, to ensure that the symbolic objects which showed where the action was taking place should appear to the spectator to exist in three dimensions. There was no occasion for crude realism in this transference from a liturgical to a dramatic mode of expression. Nonetheless, within the limits of an almost Aristotelian denial of chance and movement, it insisted that the optical laws governing illusion should not be ignored.

Giotto had no thought of being true to life. Yet only a few years after his death he was praised by Boccaccio for his skill in depicting reality. "Nature never made anything that he did not imitate or even reproduce in paint, so that men who see his work are often deluded into taking the painted for the real." Boccaccio's reality, of course, was not transcendent reality, and by nature he only meant outward appearance.

Meanwhile, Italian patrons had become inquisitive about the nature of things, and they now expected artists to give them a genuine illustration of reality. In this connection another attitude made itself felt. One could hardly call it bourgeois without slandering its most fervent hopes; yet it was an attitude common, not only to practitioners of medicine, law and government, but to all those who had done well in trade and had risen to power in the urban aristocracy. These patricians had not been to a university, but they had learned to use their eyes with the keenness essential for estimating at a glance the quality of the innumerable commodities of *mercatura*. The ramifications of their business compelled them to see the world plainly and to see it whole. They understood figures, and to them the word *ratio* also meant a bookkeeping transaction. Men like these wanted painted scenes to mirror reality more faithfully while preserving the logic, unity and spaciousness of the stage. Allegories of Good Government were, of course, conceptual and had an abstract setting; but at the lower and more prosaic level of vulgar curiosities, there appeared at Siena the first logically planned landscape. It was commissioned by a town council composed of merchants and businessmen just at the time when Giovanni Villani was using the accurate instruments of statistics to describe Florence.

After the plague epidemic of 1348-1350 had wrought its havoc, the Sienese landscape, as created by Ambrogio Lorenzetti in his frescoes in the town hall, was taken as a model by the image-carvers of Lombardy. Then, having traveled from Milan to Paris, it enabled the Limbourg brothers, who themselves had inherited the incomplete but more sensual realism of chivalry, to make a true portrait of the fair countenance of France.

THE FACE OF NATURE

The walls of royal apartments were concealed by tapestries or frescoes bidding the inmates go forth in pursuit of happiness, whether the zest of battle and the chase or the tranquil converse of an arbor. For his private rooms in the Wardrobe Tower at Avignon Pope Clement VI chose scenes of fishponds and the cool shade of noble trees. French painters were already working on these under the direction of Robin de Romans when, in 1343, Matteo Giovannetti da Viterbo was summoned to the papal court. While the Italian artist may have helped to complete these charming landscapes, it may well be that the great Sienese, Simone Martini, who was still living, was mainly responsible for them. The fresco is designed in successive planes, so that it recedes into a genuinely distant background. A little earlier Simone had used the same visual technique for the pastoral scenes of his Virgil *in the Ambrosian Library.*

Illustrators, in fact, were much given to depicting open-air life. Breviaries, especially, always began with a calendar of sacred festivals, which enabled artists to depict, month by month, the changing countenance of nature. The old, rural aristocracy of France regarded May as the month when the love of life was strongest and men shared in the triumphant rebirth of the countryside. May was the month of adventure, for then the grass was rich enough to provide pasture for lengthy forays. It was also the month of lovemaking, when village maidens would dance in the meadows. Elsewhere the Master of the Rohan Hours uttered the most pitiable of cries to lay bare all the suffering and sorrow of man; but for May he depicted the Heavenly Twins with the purity of a classical intaglio. This month was traditionally symbolized by riders on mettlesome steeds, and the horseman in the Rohan Hours *is the very incarnation of youthful gaiety as he canters into the greenwood, a spray of lily-of-the-valley in his hand.*

Man is not so closely wedded to nature in the landscapes by the Limbourg brothers. They are no longer depicted as a labyrinth, through whose web of mysterious apertures the eye is led from one discovery or surprise to another, until it encounters the blue, enclosing canopy of sky. Far from observing phenomena with the infinite detail of Occamist cosmogony, they present a vision of nature in its fullness, at once monistic and immeasurable. By their play of light the painters of the Très Riches Heures *have given their landscapes the authenticity of the world around them. It is a world no longer fragmented by abstract, analytical reasoning, but illuminated so that men may see it in the round.*

MASTER OF THE ROHAN HOURS. THE MONTH OF MAY, ABOUT 1418.
MINIATURE FROM THE CALENDAR OF "LES GRANDES HEURES DU DUC DE ROHAN," MS LAT. 9471, BIBLIOTHÈQUE NATIONALE, PARIS.

THE TRIUMPH OF DEATH, DETAIL: PARTY OF PLEASURE-SEEKERS IN A GROVE, ABOUT 1350. FRESCO IN THE CAMPO SANTO, PISA.

FISHING SCENE, 1343-1347. FRESCO IN THE CHAMBRE DE LA GARDEROBE, PALACE OF THE POPES, AVIGNON.

Côment nature voulant orendroit plus
que onques mes reueler z faire esclaircir
les biens z honneurs qui sont en amours
vient a Guille de machaut z li ordene z en
charge afaire sur ce nouueaux dis amou
reux. et li baille pour li conseillier z aidier
a ce faire trois de ses enfans. Cest asauoir
Sens. Retorique z musique. et li dit
par ceste maniere

IE nature par qui tout est fourme
Quanque a ca ius z sur terre z en mer
Uieng et toy Guille qui fourme
Tay a part pour faire par toy fourmer
Nouueaux dis amoureux plaisant
Pour ce te bail et trois de mes enfans
Qui ten donront la pratique
Et se tu mes deux trois bien cognoissans
Nome sont Sens Retorique musique

WORKS OF GUILLAUME DE MACHAUT: GUILLAUME DE MACHAUT RECEIVING "NATURE," ABOUT 1370.
FOLIO E, MS FR. 1584, BIBLIOTHÈQUE NATIONALE, PARIS.

208

THE LIMBOURG BROTHERS. THE MONTH OF DECEMBER, ABOUT 1415.
MINIATURE FROM THE CALENDAR OF THE "TRÈS RICHES HEURES DU DUC DE BERRY," MS 1284, MUSÉE CONDÉ, CHANTILLY.

THE GENERATION OF 1420

At the approach of what the historians of European civilization call the Renaissance, both Paris and Rome were eclipsed by the new schools of artists in Florence and Flanders. At Rome the Papacy was floundering in the mire of schism, while in France the Valois court was convulsed and exhausted by family quarrels, civil disorder and war. These political vicissitudes did not emancipate the artist from his royal patrons, who continued to control him as firmly as they had done throughout the fourteenth century. It is true that Tuscany and Flanders now possessed the richest towns in the world; but in their heyday Paris, Avignon and Milan, the nurseries of courtly art, had been the most populous and thriving of great cities. Like the Limbourg brothers, Jan van Eyck was a court painter and body-servant to a prince. Though he sometimes worked for businessmen, they too belonged to a prince's household. They took pride in the fact and echoed their master's tastes. The Dukes of Burgundy, those princes of the royal house who had succeeded to the fame and fortune of the Kings of France, established themselves in Flanders, where they set up their court and attracted to it the finest artists who could no longer find work in Paris. It was thanks to their patronage that Flemish painting ceased to be provincial and suddenly took the lead in artistic discovery. The golden age of Florence began when the ravages of pestilence among her aristocracy had been repaired and her leading citizens, heirs to a culture inspired by knightly ideals, once more constituted a well-ordered society. The new forms of art germinated in Florence at the very moment when the Republic was imperceptibly turning into a principality; when the tyrant whose sons later tried to represent him as a paragon among patrons was already tightening his grip on the Seigniory. At Bruges and in Tuscany the Church was no less influential in 1420 than it had been in the past; but neither had its power increased, and art continued to be exactly what the monarch wanted. The geographical change, without implying any break in tradition, did put an end to the attempt at a uniformly Gothic style. Instead it revealed two divergent tendencies which from now on became sharply contrasted.

At the Burgundian court in Dijon and later in the Low Countries, sculpture took the initiative before painting. The same was true of Florence, where a hundred years earlier Nicola Pisano had led the way for Giotto. But it was the painters Van Eyck and Masaccio who completed the process. William of Occam's analytical vision, with its insistence on the discreteness of each object, received a razor-like trenchancy from the brush of Van Eyck. Yet he followed the Limbourg brothers in so focusing the objects he observed as to assemble these disparate phenomena within a cosmos unified by the Oxford theologians' principle of light. The dreamy fantasies of chivalry were dispelled by this light. It was the Pentecostal fire, the light which had illumined the mystics of Groenendael and which the Cologne school of painters had tried to reproduce in their mystical gardens. The surrounding wall of shadow; the flickering reflections of mirrors and precious stones in the peaceful seclusion of a closet; the iridescence caused by a shaft of light in the open air: by such means could reality be portrayed with harmony and truth. Masaccio, meanwhile, was reverting to the stately mode of Giotto in order to express an austere, Stoic Christianity, measured and self-controlled, for which neither fantasy nor mystic illumination would suffice. He eschewed the decorative profusion of arabesques and cared little about the appearance of things or the way they were lit. Tuscany was a land of architects, who loved the sobriety of plain surfaces and the chaste grandeur of stone, who measured not merely objects but the emptiness of space, which they shaped with geometrical simplicity. Like them, and like Donatello who invested the faces of his Prophets with all the torments of the soul, Masaccio depicted *virtus*, whose meaning the humanists had rediscovered in Roman literature and in the massive splendor of

Imperial sculpture. His reality, unlike Van Eyck's, was an abstract, Aristotelian vision of a rational universe, seen in the clear light of logic, proportion and mathematics.

There is nonetheless an awareness of man's nobility that is common to both the Occamist Van Eyck and the Peripatetic Masaccio. Each gave pride of place to man—the New Man, in the persons of Adam and Eve. Van Eyck imbued the body of Eve with the delectable sensuousness of physical reality. With his gently rolling hills clothed in rich woodland, he created a wonderful landscape, more captivating than that in his *Adoration of the Lamb*. Similarly, Masaccio chose for his devotional theme, instead of Jesus nailed to the Cross, the doleful figures of Adam and Eve cast out of Paradise.

Yet the real innovation at this moment in the history of art must be sought elsewhere. Hitherto Jan van Eyck had worked to order, doing portraits of canons, prince-bishops and the magnates like Arnolfini who ran the Bruges offices of Florentine banking houses. Then, one day he decided to paint his wife—not as a queen or as Eve or the Virgin, but just as she was. She was no princess, and her portrait had no value for anyone except the artist himself. On that day the court painter won his independence and was free to paint what he liked. And in Florence, where Ghiberti was about to write *Commentaries* on his work, as Caesar had done on the Gallic and Civil Wars, the artist's freedom was truly manifested when there appeared in the Brancacci Chapel frescoes, amid the apostles in the *Tribute Money*, the face of Masaccio himself.

VAN EYCK - MASACCIO - DONATELLO

By the end of the fourteenth century the wealthy men for whom artists worked insisted on being able to identify the objects in a painting. Occamist nominalism, moreover, taught that no one could hope to comprehend the universe except through sensory perception of individual phenomena. In the work of the Limbourg brothers the prolonged effort to reproduce tangible lineaments culminated in visual completeness. Light, striking through the veil of atmosphere, dissolved the old, theatrical backdrop and synthesized the formerly disparate elements of a painting. It now became possible to enhance this visual unity by the use of oils, so that two-dimensional painting superseded the art of illumination. In Eve's body, which Van Eyck painted as if it were an intricate landscape, the smooth flow of light into shadow lends greater distinctness to the texture of every part. Not only does the artist pay minute attention to physical substance; he also combines discrete sensory experiences in a coherent whole, embracing every dimension of reality. Thus did the Holy Ghost unite the souls of all men in bliss beyond compare; thus did the Light shine upon the face of the waters in the act of Creation.

In Masaccio painting has indeed become a mental process. His frescoes are the offspring of architecture, an abstract, numerical art, measuring and begetting space, subduing matter to the intellect, heedless of physical likeness. The architect employs logic and mathematics to give his concept reality. The new style of Renaissance architecture, initiated in Florence by Brunelleschi, discarded Gothic luxuriance and all extraneous ornament, reverting to the pure symmetry of the church of San Miniato. Masaccio, likewise, made of emptiness, of pure, abstract space the main element in his paintings. In it he placed Man, present in the flesh. "That flesh," as Leon Battista Alberti was soon to write in his Treatise on Painting, *"would crumble to dust; but as long as breath remained to it, whoever spurned the flesh would spurn life itself." Masaccio built flesh as if it were a temple or a monument. All his figures—like the faces of the statues carved by Donatello—are imbued with the seriousness of a steadfast faith, uncompromising, rational and resolute, calmly assuming the tragic burden of man's estate.*

JAN VAN EYCK (1385/90-1441). EVE, DETAIL OF THE UPPER RIGHTHAND PANEL OF THE INTERIOR OF THE GHENT ALTARPIECE, 1430-1432. CATHEDRAL OF SAINT-BAVON, GHENT.

MASACCIO (1401-1429). ADAM AND EVE CAST OUT OF PARADISE (DETAIL), 1426-1427.
FRESCO IN THE BRANCACCI CHAPEL, SANTA MARIA DEL CARMINE, FLORENCE.

DONATELLO (ABOUT 1386-1466). THE PROPHET JEREMIAH (DETAIL), 1423-1436(?). MARBLE.
MUSEO DELL'OPERA DEL DUOMO, FLORENCE.

LIST OF ILLUSTRATIONS

PRINTED ON THE PRESSES OF
EDITIONS D'ART ALBERT SKIRA
15 FEBRUARY 1966

PHOTOGRAPHS BY

*Alinari, Florence (pages 65 right, 66, 131 top, 173/174, 174 upper right, 196), Alpenland,
Vienna (page 147 right), Archives Photographiques, Paris (page 148 right), Maurice Babey,
Basel (pages 27, 47, 48/49, 51, 57 top and bottom, 58, 59, 63, 64 top and bottom, 65 left,
81, 84/85, 111, 112, 117, 118, 119, 129, 130 bottom, 132, 136, 139, 145 left, 146 right, 156,
160/161, 168, 173 left, 188, 206, 214 and dustjacket), Carlo Bevilacqua, Milan (pages 110,
189, 215), Henry B. Beville, Alexandria, Va. (pages 141, 158), Bildarchiv Foto Marburg
(page 148 left), Robert Braunmüller, Munich (page 113), Claudio Emmer, Milan (page
49), R. B. Fleming & Co, Ltd, London (page 145 right), John R. Freeman & Co, Ltd,
London (page 26), Catherine Gardone, Dijon (page 147 left), Giraudon, Paris (pages 176 top,
185, 209), Hans Hinz, Basel (pages 48, 56), A. F. Kersting, London (pages 40 left, right,
top and bottom, 99, 102, 103, 146 left), Raymond Laniepce, Paris (page 185), Louis Loose,
Brussels (pages 101, 213), MAS, Barcelona (pages 130 top, 159), Karl H. Paulmann,
Berlin (page 42), La Photothèque, Paris (pages 23, 24, 56, 60, 72, 73, 74, 75, 76, 80, 82 top
and bottom, 113, 114, 131 bottom, 159, 167, 207), Luigi Rossi, Brescia (pages 194, 195),
Rothier, Paris (page 39 left), Scala, Florence (pages 100, 137, 169), Yan, Toulouse (page 193),
ZFA, Düsseldorf (page 187), and the photographic services of the following museums and
libraries: Berlin-Dahlem, Staatliche Museen (page 140), Milan, Biblioteca Ambrosiana
(page 71), New York, The Metropolitan Museum of Art (page 28-29), Paris, Bibliothèque
Nationale (pages 26, 41 upper right and upper left, 205, 208), Rotterdam, Museum Boymans-
Van Beuningen (page 175), Uppsala, University Library (page 174 lower right), Vienna,
Kunsthistorisches Museum (page 176 bottom), and by courtesy of Editions des Deux-Mondes,
Paris (page 25), Oxford University Press (page 41 lower right) and Österreichische
Fremdenverkehrswerbung, Vienna (page 186).*

COLOR PLATES ENGRAVED BY GUEZELLE & RENOUARD, PARIS

BLACK AND WHITE PLATES BY IMPRIMERIES RÉUNIES, LAUSANNE

PRINTED IN SWITZERLAND